Actionable Agile Metrics
for Predictability

An Introduction

Daniel S. Vacanti

Actionable Agile Metrics for Predictability

An Introduction

Daniel S. Vacanti

This book is for sale at
http://leanpub.com/actionableagilemetrics

This version was published on 2015-08-10

ISBN 978-0-9864363-3-8

Leanpub

This is a Leanpub book. Leanpub empowers authors and publishers with the Lean Publishing process. Lean Publishing is the act of publishing an in-progress ebook using lightweight tools and many iterations to get reader feedback, pivot until you have the right book and build traction once you do.

To Ann, Skye, Sicily, and Manhattan: the only measures of value in my life.

Contents

CONTENTS

Preface

Your process is unpredictable. What you may not realize, though, is that you are the one responsible for making it that way. But that is not necessarily your fault. You have been taught to collect the wrong metrics, implement the wrong policies, and make the wrong decisions. Together, we can do better.

Up until now you have probably assumed that the reason your process is unpredictable is due to circumstances completely outside of your control. However, you have much more control over the way you work than you think you do. Whether explicit or not, you have put policies in place that specifically prevent you from being predictable. Amongst other things you start new work at a faster rate than you finish old work, you work on too many items at the same time, you ignore systemic dependencies and impediments, and you expedite requests that do not need to be expedited. You, in effect, initiate a denial of service attack on yourself, and then wonder why it takes so long for things to get things done.

But all of those policies are under your control.

If we, as knowledge workers, want to get to a predictable world, we must first start by controlling the policies we can control. Taking this control will seem uncomfortable at first. It will mean saying no to customer requests to start new work immediately. It will mean placing much less emphasis on upfront estimation and planning. It will mean looking at a different set of metrics than the ones you have been trained to track. Those metrics will tell you how predictable you are and what actions to take to improve. If you choose to collect the metrics suggested by this book, you will see that the data provided by them will immediately reflect policies you have in place. That data will in turn suggest the changes to your policies necessary to be more predictable. Those policy changes will themselves be reflected in the new data you collect after the change. And so on and so on.

Your process is unpredictable. You know it. Your customers know it. Now it is time to do something about it.

Why Write this Book?

Because our customers demand predictability. Because you need someone on your side who has been asked tough questions and has found a way to give meaningful answers. Because most organizations that I visit are either uninformed or have been misinformed about what metrics and analytics they need to track to be predictable.

But to get you where you need to be, I am going to ask you provocative questions. I am going to challenge your assumptions about what true Agility is. I may make you uncomfortable with some of the conclusions that I draw. I hope you will forgive me for all of these as my only intention is to make your process better. After all, as I just said, I am on your side.

Who Should Read this Book

Anyone who has ever been asked to give an estimate should read this book. Likewise, anyone who has ever asked for an estimate should read this book.

Analysts, developers and testers need to know how to stop giving estimates and how to start making accurate predictions.

Product owners, project managers, and executives need to know what makes for a meaningful prediction and how to hold teams accountable to make those predictions.

Conventions Used

All metrics and analytics will be capitalized. For example: Work In Progress, Cycle Time, Throughput, Cumulative Flow Diagram, Scatterplot, etc.

I am also going to capitalize all methodology names. For example: Agile, Scrum, Kanban, etc.

Lastly, I am going to use the words "process" and "system" interchangeably. I will try to make the distinction clear when a distinction is necessary.

How to Read

This book is intended to be read in order as the concepts in later chapters are built on the concepts developed in earlier ones. However, each chapter can stand alone, and, where possible, when I re-examine a concept that has already been explained, I will try to reference the part of the book that contains the more detailed explanation.

PART ONE – FLOW FOR PREDICTABILITY

Chapter 1 defines my notion of predictability. It introduces the metrics that are necessary to track to become predictable, and it will explain what it means to turn those metrics into actionable interventions.

Chapter 2 is a detailed discussion of the basic metrics of flow. The rest of the book will assume knowledge of what those metrics are and how they are defined.

Chapter 3 is an introduction to Little's Law. If you want to be predictable, you have to understand why Little's Law works. Period.

PART TWO – CUMULATIVE FLOW DIAGRAMS FOR PREDICTABILITY

Chapter 4 is an in depth explanation of what Cumulative Flow Diagrams (CFDs) are and what they are not. This chapter is a must read because most previous agile publications that deal with CFDs are erroneous and most agile electronic tools build them incorrectly. I will attempt to remedy all of that.

Chapter 5 explains how to read all of the basic metrics of flow off of a CFD. The ability to read these metrics is one of the biggest reasons to use CFDs in the first place.

Chapter 6 explains how to interpret the results of a generated CFD. Many common patterns that appear in CFDs are explained.

Chapter 7 begins the exploration of the assumptions behind Little's Law and CFDs by looking at process arrivals and departures. If you get these right then you have gone a long way toward predictability. Not inconsequentially, arrivals and departures represents the first part of a principle known as the Conservation of Flow

Chapter 8 continues the discussion of Little's Law's assumptions by looking at the second part of the principle of Conservation of Flow. This second part explains why just-in-time commitments and just-in-time prioritization is possible and necessary for predictability.

Chapter 9 introduces the little-known concept of Flow Debt, how to see it on a CFD, and why it kills predictability. What actions to take when it accumulates are also discussed.

PART THREE – CYCLE TIME SCATTERPLOTS FOR PREDICTABILITY

Chapter 10 is an in depth examination of the second most important analytical chart: the Cycle Time Scatterplot.

Chapter 11 explains how to interpret a Cycle Time Scatterplot. Many common patterns that appear on Scatterplots are explained.

Chapter 12 introduces one of the least known and least understood practices needed for predictability: the Cycle Time Service Level Agreement (SLA). Some thoughts on how to set SLAs and manage to them are explored.

PART FOUR – PUTTING IT ALL TOGETHER FOR PREDICTABILITY

Chapter 13 explores pull policies and how those policies are one of the main sources of variability in your process.

Chapter 14 presents a survey of some forecasting techniques and the pros and cons of each.

Chapter 15 is my take on some of the advantages and pitfalls of the Monte Carlo Method as they pertain to predictability.

Chapter 16 presents a short guide on how to get started and outlines some pitfalls to watch out for as you begin. If you get overwhelmed with your own data initiative, this chapter is a good place to start.

PART FIVE – A CASE STUDY FOR PREDICTABILITY

Chapter 17 re-examines a previously published case study from Siemens Health Services. This case study has been updated with an emphasis on how Siemens put into practice all of the principles in this book.

There is another disclaimer I should mention up front. The concepts in the book are based on the principles of flow. What flow is and how to achieve it is a topic for a whole book in itself, so I will not spend much time on those definitions. I refer you to the work of Don Reinertsen and some of the other authors listed in the

Bibliography for a more detailed discussion of flow.

Also, I believe the concepts presented throughout are relevant regardless of your chosen Agile implementation. Where applicable, I will try to point out how actions might differ based on a specific Agile methodology.

Lastly, this book has a distinct software development bent to it, but you need not be in the software product development industry nor do you need to be familiar with any Agile methodology to understand these principles. They can be equally applied to any process regardless of domain.

ActionableAgile.com

Finally, and unless otherwise noted, all of the images of the analytics charts and graphs that are presented in this book were built using the ActionableAgile™ Analytics tool. This tool is one that my company has developed and can be found at:

 https://www.actionableagile.com

You can find a fully functional free demo of the tool at:

 https://www.actionableagile.com/analytics-demo

And you can sign-up for a free trial version of the tool for use with your own data at:

 https://www.actionableagile.com/cms/analytics-free-trial-signup.html

In addition to the tool, accompanying blog posts, book updates and errata, videos, etc. can also be found at the ActionableAgile™ website.

PART ONE - FLOW FOR PREDICTABILITY

Chapter 1 - Flow, Flow Metrics, and Predictability

I first met Bennet Vallet in the spring of 2012. At the time, Bennet was a Director of Product Development for Siemens Health Services (HS) located just outside of Philadelphia, Pennsylvania. We met one night at an Agile Philly event where I was giving a talk on the principles of flow. He came up to me after my presentation and asked if we could set up some time later to discuss the problems he was facing at HS. Of course I agreed.

We spoke on the phone the following day and during that call Bennet outlined his thoughts on all the issues he was facing at HS. Those issues are fully documented in the case study presented in Chapter 17 so I will not go into any detail here. Suffice it to say, however, that toward the end of the call, I suggested to Bennet that to fix these problems we must first consider what is most important to his customers. In other words, if I were to speak to his customers, what would they tell me were the three most important things to them?

"Oh, that's easy," Bennet replied. "The three most important things to our customers are predictability, predictability, and predictability."

Predictability

"When will it be done?"

That is the first question your customers ask you once you start work for them. And, for the most part, it is the only thing they are interested in until you deliver.

Whether your process is predictable or not is judged by the accuracy of your answer. Think about how many times you have been asked that question and think how many times you have been wrong.

Now think about some of the practices you have put in place to come up with your answer. Maybe you have an Agile methodology you are fond of. Maybe you prefer a more traditional project management approach. But are either of those practices actually helping?

As a case in point, Bennet had been working with mature Agile teams for a long time, and those teams had been adhering to established Agile practices. In his mind he was doing everything right, so he reasonably believed that predictability would inevitably follow. Yet he constantly struggled to accurately answer the most important questions that his customers were asking.

To illustrate why Bennet struggled (and why you probably struggle as well), I would like you to look through the following set of questions and see if one or more apply to your current situation: - Are you constantly asked to start new work before you have had a chance to finish old work? - Are you constantly asked to expedite new requests in addition to being expected to get all of your other current work done according to original estimates and commitments? - How many features do you start but do not finish because they get cancelled while you are working on them? How likely is it that the new items that replace the cancelled work will themselves get cancelled? - When something that you are working on gets blocked (for whatever reason), do you simply put that blocked work aside and start to work on something new? - Do your estimates give consideration to how many other items will be in progress at the time you start work? - Do you ignore the order in which you work on items currently in progress? -

Do you constantly add new scope or acceptance criteria to items in progress because it is easier to modify an existing feature rather than to open a new one? - When an item takes too long to complete, have you ever said or heard someone say "it is just bigger than we thought it was" and/or "it will get done when it gets done"? - When things take too long to complete, is management's first response always to have the team work overtime?

I could list many more, but the point is that these behaviors are symptomatic of something seriously wrong with your process. Regrettably, your chosen project management framework (including any Agile methodology you may be using) may be perpetuating the underlying illness. When it comes to unpredictability, the thing that really ails you is a lack of flow.

Flow and the Basic Metrics of Flow

Simply stated, flow is the movement and delivery of customer value through a process. In knowledge work, our whole reason for existence is to deliver value to the customer. Therefore, it stands to reason that our whole process should be oriented around optimizing flow.

If your process is unpredictable, the first thing to investigate is poor flow. A telltale sign of a suboptimal flow is a large buildup of work somewhere in your process. This buildup of work is most commonly called a "queue". Large queues generally mean no flow.

Queues form when work items that have been started just get stuck somewhere in your process (without completing). Items may get stuck because: - There are no more resources available to continue working on them. - Some manager mandates that more new work be started before current work has finished. - Resources that are actually doing the work are constantly pulled in multiple different directions and are not allowed to focus on any one thing. - There is a dependency on some external team or vendor.

Work may get stuck for all of those reasons and more. Management of flow, therefore, usually begins by attempting to "unstick" stuck work.

Unfortunately, your project management framework makes you blind to queues. You are blind to them because you are never asked to look for them in the first place. If you are doing some sort of Agile, then you might assume that iterations or sprints insulate you from large queues. However, if you answered "yes" to any of the questions I asked above, then there is a good chance you have a large buildup of work somewhere in your process.

Even though you do not see these large queues, you are constantly feeling their effect. The most obvious effect that you feel is that work takes too long to complete. Traditional project management responses to elongated completion times might be to constantly refigure project plans, to continuously revisit resource assignments, and to force teams to work overtime. Not only do those actions not solve the core problem, but in most instances they tend to make things worse.

But what if we could see these problems before they happen? What if we could take action to prevent them from happening in the first place? That is where actionable metrics come in.

Actionable Metrics for Predictability

The best way to fix the problem of large queues is not to allow them to form in the first place. To do that we must somehow measure our queues. The best way to measure a queue is to simply count the number of items you are working on at any given time. When that number gets too big then no new work gets started until something old has finished. The total count of items currently being worked on is the flow metric commonly known as Work In Progress.

As I just mentioned, the direct consequence of large buildup of work is that all of that queued work itself takes longer to complete. The flow metric that represents how long it takes for work to complete is called Cycle Time. Cycle Time ultimately answers the question of "When will it be done?" A process with elongated Cycle Times makes it harder to answer that question.

The direct consequence of elongated Cycle Times is a decrease in Throughput. Throughput is the metric that represents how much work completes per unit of time. A decrease in Throughput therefore means that less work is getting done. The less work that gets done, the less value we deliver.

To manage flow we are going to need to closely monitor those three metrics:

1. **Work In Progress** (the number of items that we are working on at any given time),
2. **Cycle Time** (how long it takes each of those items to get through our process), and
3. **Throughput** (how many of those items complete per unit of time).

The rest of this book will explain that if your process is not predictable, or is veering away from predictability, these metrics will suggest specific interventions that you can make to get back on track. In a word, these metrics are actionable.

Actionable Metrics for Predictability: The set of metrics that will suggest specific interventions that will result in the outcomes you are expecting.

Once we know what metrics to track, we can visualize those metrics in flow-based analytics. These analytics will bring visibility to any problems with flow much more quickly so that we can proactively deal with issues rather than retroactively fight fires.

Items taking too long? Not enough getting done? These metrics and analytics will give us some of the magic levers we can pull to make things better.

Why These Metrics

In addition to being actionable, there are certain other criteria that must be met when deciding what metrics to capture. Eric Reis, of Lean Startup fame, gives one perspective: "The only metrics that entrepreneurs should invest in are those that help them make decisions." Well said. Troy Magennis, of Lean Forecasting fame, goes even further: "If a metric does not offer predictive power, then capturing that metric is waste." I discussed earlier how the important questions that our customers ask are going to require us to make predictions. I have further suggested that these flow metrics in and of themselves are the answers to those questions. By definition, then, tracking these metrics offer predictive power and will help us make better decisions.

Yet another vital criterion exists that should be considered when determining what metrics to capture: cost. There is no point in tracking a metric if it is going to bankrupt you to do so. Herein lies yet another advantage of tracking these metrics of flow: these metrics are very inexpensive to gather. Any Agile tool should track these metrics (how easy it is to mine this data from a given tool and how accurately those tools display the analytics is a different story that we will get to in Chapter 16). Even if you do not have an Agile tool, these metrics are very easy to manually track using a simple spreadsheet. WIP, Cycle Time, and Throughput take very little time to collect, and offer the biggest bang for the buck in terms of gaining precious insight into the overall health, performance, and predictability of your process.

Why Not Traditional Agile Metrics?

For the most part, the types of actionable metrics and analytics to be discussed in this book do not exist in traditional Agile guidance and traditional methodologies. They do not exist because, as I discussed earlier, most of those earlier methodologies were not designed from the premise that managing flow is the best strategy for predictability. Further, traditional Agile metrics and analytics give no visibility nor any suggestion of what to do when things go wrong. "Work Harder", "Estimate Better", "Plan Better", "Hope", "Pray", "Cry" are not viable nor sustainable strategies.

Adding to this problem is that all of the tooling that has been developed around these legacy Agile metrics provide incorrect or incomplete information. In the absence of a tool to do it for them, a team's only option is to manually track flow metrics and build the corresponding analytics themselves. However, most teams do not want to invest in manually collecting new types of data when they have already made an investment in their current toolset. Therefore these metrics never get collected and the proper analytics never get built. Because of these points, even when presented with the correct metrics, most teams do not know how to interpret or take action on them.

What Makes these Metrics Lean and Agile?

To begin with a counterexample, it is incomprehensible to me that metrics like Story Points and Velocity are accepted as Agile. I am being purposefully provocative here, but those metrics—and the corresponding analytics like Burn Down charts—are about as far from Agile as one can get. Let's explore why for a second.

Part of the Agile Manifesto mentions "Customer Collaboration". I fully support that notion that our work should involve close collaboration with the customer. However, to me, collaboration means speaking the language of the customer. And that language should extend to cover all the metrics and analytics that we use. Have you ever had to explain what a Story Point is to a customer? How about Velocity? If you do not like yourself very much, march into your CFO's office someday and try to explain what a Story Point is.

However, I guarantee all of your stakeholders understand the concept of elapsed time. I guarantee they understand the concept of the total number of features to be delivered in a release. If we truly want to be Agile, we are going to have to adopt the language of our customers. To that end, we must choose words and concepts that they are comfortable with—not force them to learn a new, arbitrary, and unhelpful vocabulary.

Additionally, one of the key tenants of Lean is respect for people. To demonstrate why flow and flow metrics are Lean, I would like you to try the following experiment at home sometime (if you have a spouse or partner). I have a wife so I will explain it with her in mind. In this experiment, I would start by asking my wife to do something for me. The particular task I ask her to do does not really matter as long as it will take a non-trivial amount of time to complete. Before she is finished I will ask her to stop what she is working on to do something else for me. Before she is finished with that new task, I will ask her to stop and do something else. At some point after I have requested her to do the third or fourth thing I will ask her why she is not finished with the first thing I requested and why it is taking so long. I will continue to do this until the nearest blunt instrument she beats me to death with is marked as "Prosecution's Exhibit A".

The Solution to Poor Predictability

Today's economic climate has caused a heated competition for companies to acquire customers, retain them, and deliver the products they want when they want them.

You know this all too well because you bear the brunt of this heated competition; because you are expected to create, manage, and maintain the products that customers desire; because you are expected to reduce the time and resources needed to launch products quickly to meet ever-changing customer demands.

Solving these problems will require a new strategy. That new strategy is to focus on the management of flow. A focus on flow necessitates not only a shift in thinking (away from capacity utilization and estimation and planning) but also a shift in the quantities used to evaluate process performance (away from ideal hours, level of effort, points, velocity, etc.)

That is where the metrics of flow come in. Observing and measuring flow is going to provide the missing component that you need to make your process more predictable. If you can get to a process that has stable, predictable flow, then the act of estimating and planning—the act of making predictions—becomes trivial. The measurement of flow and its resultant metrics will take care of all that for us.

I began this chapter by talking about Bennet's predictability problems at HS. In the months that followed our first meeting in Philadelphia, I had the great opportunity to work with Bennet and to reflect with him on the relationship between flow and predictability. During one of those conversations, Bennet said, "You know, most people think of predictability as a noun. It's not. It's a verb." Exactly right. It is not that you *are* predictable or *are not* predictable. It is that you "do" predictability. Predictability is proactive and not reactive. The actions you take today have the biggest impact on your predictability tomorrow.

Key Learnings and Takeaways

- To get more predictable in knowledge work, we must abandon old project management paradigms and adopt new ones. The new paradigm we must adopt is the focus on and the management of flow.
- A lack of flow manifests itself as a buildup of work (large queues of work). The best way to fix the problem of large queues is not to allow them to form in the first place.
- Managing for flow necessitates a new, different

set of metrics than traditional project management frameworks would ever prescribe or suggest.

- Observing and measuring the metrics of flow is the true path to predictability.
- Flow metrics are defined in the language of the customer and are the proper metrics to track in order to be lean and agile.
- Flow metrics will suggest the actionable interventions needed to make us more predictable.

Chapter 2 - The Basic Metrics of Flow

As I discussed in the previous chapter, understanding flow and managing for it requires a different paradigm than that espoused by traditional processes and frameworks. The answers to the essential questions of predictable process execution are not found in project plans, resource utilization charts, or team members' estimates. The answers will come from the monitoring, measurement, and management of a specific set of metrics. This chapter is all about defining these metrics: Work In Progress (WIP), Cycle Time, and Throughput.

The good news is that these flow metrics are exactly the ones we need to track in order to answer the questions that our customers are asking. The customer question "How long to complete?" is best answered by the flow metric known as Cycle Time. The customer question "How many new features am I going to get in the next release?" is a question best answered by the flow metric known as Throughput. The last of the three, Work In Progress (WIP), does not directly answer any particular customer question, but it is the metric that will most greatly influence the other two. For that reason, I will start this discussion with it.

Work In Progress

Work In Progress is the most important flow metric to track for two reasons. First, as we will see in the coming chapters, WIP is the best predictor of overall system performance. Second, the other two metrics of flow—Cycle Time and Throughput—will themselves both be defined in terms of WIP.

Even so, WIP is probably the hardest metric to define. That is because the definition of WIP is two dimensional: it must cover both the notion of "work" and the notion of "in progress".

Let's look at the idea of *work* first. For the purposes of this book, I regard any direct or indirect discrete unit of customer value as a candidate for *work*. The generic term I will use for these candidate units of customer value is "work item". A work item might be a user story, an epic, a feature, or a project. It might be a requirement, use case, or enhancement. How you capture work as work items and how name your work items is entirely up to you.

Secondly, to define *in progress* we must first consider the boundaries of your process. To do so, let's use the metaphor of a simple queuing system. I would argue that all processes can be modelled in the manner depicted in Figure 2.1:

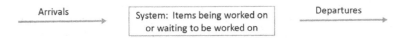

Figure 2.1: A Simple Queuing System

In a queuing system there is work that arrives to a process and there is work that departs a process. When making a determination of whether something counts as in progress or not, the first aspect of system that needs to be considered is what does it mean for something to have "arrived"? That is to say, your team needs to define a specific point where a unit of work transforms from being just some arbitrary idea into being a legitimate work item that is to immediately be acted on and completed. Before that arrival point, the item is just some candidate for work. After that arrival point, the item is counted as Work In Progress.

In a pull-based system, an entry (or boundary) point is fairly easy to define. That is because in a pull system, a team only starts work when it has capacity to do so. Thus, a work item can only count as Work In Progress if it has been voluntarily pulled into the process by the individual, team, or organization responsible for operating that process. The "arrival point" of the system, therefore, is the point at which the team performs its first pull transaction on the work. After that first pull transaction, an item is considered WIP until it departs the process. (This arrival point is also considered a point of "commitment". An in-depth look at how just-in-time commitment and just-in-time prioritization work are topics that I will cover in Chapter 8).

For push-based systems, an entry point is much harder to define. That is because there is no consideration for a team's capacity when deciding when work should be started. In a push system work can be considered started when any stakeholder has a reasonable expectation that work has been committed to (whether the team responsible for performing the work knows about it or agrees to it or not). This expectation could be set for such arbitrary reasons as the work has been requested, the project has been funded, or some manager somewhere thinks it is a good idea to start—regardless of whether there is any capacity to do so.

Obviously I have a bias for pull systems over push systems, but the concept of WIP applies regardless of context. If you find yourself operating within a push system, then the best, first predictability exercise you might want to undertake is to define the boundaries around your process. Getting a handle on what you consider WIP is a necessary (but unfortunately not sufficient) step down the road to predictability.

For a work item to no longer count as in progress, there must be a specific point of departure from the process. Departure could be defined as delivery to an actual end user or delivery to some other downstream team or process. For example, if a development team is responsible for its own deployments to production, then that team might consider an item only to have departed once a deployment to production has been made. Or a different team who is not responsible for deployments might consider an item to only have departed once it has been reasonably handed off to a downstream operations team who would then handle deployments. Again, the definition of a point of departure holds true whether you are operating a pull or a push system.

To sum up, for in progress definition purposes your team must a specific point when it considers work to have arrived to the process and it must define a specific point where work has departed the process. The definition of those two system boundaries is the crucial starting point in predictable process design. Once you have made those decisions, then all work items between those two points will count as Work In Progress:

 WIP: All discrete units of customer value that have entered a given process but have not exited.

If defining WIP is the hard part, then measuring it is the easy part. To calculate WIP you simply count the discrete number of work items within your process boundaries as defined above. That's it: just count.

Your natural objection might be, "doesn't that mean you have to make all of your work items the same size?" After all, the work items that come through your process are of different durations, are of disparate complexities, and may require a wide mix of resources to work on them. How can you possibly account for all of that variability and come up with a predictable system by just counting work items? While that is a reasonable question, it is not something to get hung up on.

I will spend more time on this topic a little bit later, so I am going to ask you to just suspend disbelief here and accept that when it comes to WIP and predictability, there is no requirement to have all of your work items be of the same size or complexity. There is not going to be need for any further complexity to be added to the calculation such as estimating your WIP in Story Points or assigning ideal hours to each work item. This concept is probably very uncomfortable to those of you who are used to thinking about work in terms of relative complexity or level of effort. As I mentioned in the introduction, you need to abandon that type of thinking if you truly want to build predictable processes.

For those of you who do not want to wait, an explanation of why size does not matter (said the actress to the bishop) will be given in Chapter 3 (the chapter on Little's Law). For now, all you need to know is that WIP is calculated by counting individual work items.

Nor is there any restriction on the level at which you track work items. You can track WIP at the portfolio, project, feature, epic, or story level—just to name a few. All of these types of decisions will be completely up to you.

For you Kanban practitioners out there, you will also want to note that there is a difference between WIP and WIP limits. You cannot calculate WIP simply by adding up all the WIP limits on your board. It should work that way, but it does not. This result should be obvious as most Kanban boards do not always have columns that are at their full WIP limit. A more common situation is to have a Kanban board with WIP limit violations in multiple columns. In either of those cases simply adding up WIP limits will not give you an accurate WIP calculation. Even in a Kanban world, you still have to actively track the total number of work items in your process.

An implication of all of this is that most often items located in a backlog do not meet the definition of being included in a WIP calculation. There is a subtlety here that is going to require further discussion as it refers to the "point of commitment" that I mentioned a little earlier (for this deeper discussion, please see Chapter 8). Just know that—for the most part—when I talk about WIP, I do not include backlog items in that discussion.

As an interesting aside, you should know that you will have the option to segment and report on your WIP as you see fit. In some contexts it may be beneficial to lump all of your WIP together and examine it from a holistic system's view. Or it may be beneficial to segment that WIP into types or categories and examine each one of those subgroups on its own.

For example, let's say your team performs work for the sales department, the marketing department, and the finance department. Let's also say that your team is responsible for maintenance on a variety of existing applications. When looking at WIP you may want to combine all of those requests together into one big group.

Or your team may choose to just look at the part of your WIP that pertains to sales. Or your team may choose to look at the part of your WIP that pertains to marketing. Or you may just want to look at how your maintenance items are doing. From a metrics perspective, performing that type segmentation is not only going to be perfectly okay, but also, as mentioned earlier, in some instances is going to be desirable. If your team does segment WIP into different categories, then it is also going to be valid to talk about the Cycle Time and Throughput of those different type segments. Segmenting (or filtering) WIP into different types may also be important from a reporting and analytics perspective which is why I will revisit this topic in the flow analytics chapters to come (Chapter 5 and Chapter 10).

Not only are the other two metrics of flow defined in terms of WIP, but—it turns out—those other two are also best predicted by WIP. This result is so important that I am going to dedicate much of the following chapters to it. My point here is only to suggest that if your team ever wants to have any hope of operating a predictable process, then you are going to have to get control of WIP. If you are not currently tracking WIP, then you are going to want to start. Sooner is better than later.

Cycle Time

As I mentioned in Chapter 1, the first question our customers ask when we start work for them is "When will it be done?" Answering that question will require us to measure the flow metric of Cycle Time. Measuring Cycle Time becomes much easier now that you have a basic understanding of WIP.

In the previous section I stated that a process has

specific arrival and departure boundaries and that any item of customer value between those two boundaries can reasonably be counted as WIP. Once your team determines the points of delineation that define Work In Progress, the definition of Cycle Time becomes very easy:

 Cycle Time: The amount of elapsed time that a work item spends as Work In Progress.

This definition is based on one offered by Hopp and Spearman in their Factory Physics book and, I believe, holds up well in most knowledge work contexts. Defining Cycle Time in terms of WIP removes much—if not all—of the arbitrariness of some of the other explanations of Cycle Time that you may have seen (and been confused by) and gives us a tighter definition to start measuring this metric. The moral of this story is: you essentially have control over when something is counted as Work In Progress in your process. Take some time to define those policies around what it means for an item to be "Work In Progress" in your system and start and stop your Cycle Time clock accordingly.

Not only does defining Cycle Time in terms of Work In Progress make it more concrete and easier for people to understand, but it also brings some needed consistency when talking about Cycle Time with respect to Little's Law (Chapter 3) and with respect to how Cycle Time is (or is not!) visualized on a Cumulative Flow Diagram (Chapter 5).

Lastly, notice the emphasis on "elapsed time". The use of elapsed time is probably very different from the guidance you have previously been given. Most other methodologies ask you to measure only the actual amount of time spent actively working on a given item (if they ask you to measure time at all). I happen to think this guidance is wrong. I have a couple of reasons why.

First, and most importantly, your customers probably think about the world in terms of elapsed time. For example, let's say that on March 1, you communicate to your customers that something will be done in 30 days. My guess would be that your customer's expectation would be that they would get their item on or before March 31. However, if you meant 30 "business days" then *your* expectation is the customer would get something sometime around the middle of April. I am sure you can see where that difference in expectations might be a problem.

Second, if you only measure active time, you are ignoring a large part of your predictability problem. It is the time that an item spends waiting or delayed (i.e., *not* actively being worked) that is usually where most of your unpredictability lies. It is precisely that area that we are going to look at for most substantial predictability improvements. Remember, delay is the enemy of flow!

Lead Time vs. Cycle Time

If you have been exposed to Lean or Kanban concepts before reading this book, then what I have just defined as Cycle Time may sound a lot like what you have come to recognize as Lead Time. I understand that most people in the Kanban community prefer the term Lead Time to Cycle Time, but I am not one of them. My intention here is not to dive headlong into an academic (and ultimately useless) debate about which nomenclature is better, but

I feel that I should at least present my thoughts on why I have chosen the terms that I have. You may agree or disagree with my reasoning, but I hope you understand my intention here is not to be provocative or antagonistic (yet). I am going to talk about nomenclature in general a little later, but these specific terms require some special attention.

So why choose the term Cycle Time over Lead Time? My first argument is that regardless of whether you are talking about Cycle Time or Lead Time, you still have to qualify the boundaries of your time calculation. That is do say, both terms are very dependent on one's perspective: one person's Lead Time is another person's Cycle Time and vice versa. For example, the development team's Lead Time is just the Product Manager's Cycle Time through the development phase. While it is true that Lead Time gives more of a sense of an end-to-end calculation, what "end-to-end" means must still be defined for any given context. Given that in both cases boundaries must be qualified, I see no clear advantage of the term Lead Time over the term Cycle Time. Further, defining Cycle Time in terms of when something is counted as WIP clears up a lot of this ambiguity.

Secondly, I do not buy the argument that we, the Lean-Agile community, should shy away from using the term Cycle Time because the manufacturing industry has already defined it in a different way that may or may not be in agreement with how we use the name. I do not subscribe to the thinking that the "Lean" we are talking about here is just manufacturing theory wholly and blindly applied to knowledge work. I fully reject this thesis. The fact that manufacturing has its own definition of Cycle Time should be neither influential nor consequential to how we in knowledge work choose to define the term.

Lastly, and, I must stress, most importantly, the authors that I quote most—Reinertsen and Little— both favor the use of the term Cycle Time. If it is good enough for them, then it is good enough for me.

By the way, Hopp and Spearman also sometimes refer to Cycle Time as "Flow Time". I would suggest that the term "Flow Time" might be a better way for us to communicate what we really mean by Cycle Time in our context anyway. Even so, for the rest of the book, I will use the more common term, Cycle Time, and I will use it in the way that I have defined it here.

As I will show you in the chapter on Forecasting (Chapter 14), Cycle Time is going to be one of the main metrics you will need to come up with an accurate forecast for a project's (or story's or feature's) completion. That is to say, the reason that you want to track Cycle Time is because it provides the answer to the question, "When will it be done?" While that is certainly true, there are other important reasons to track Cycle Time.

The first supporting reason is that Cycle Time can be a rather good predictor of cost. Very generally speaking, the longer something takes to complete the more it is going to cost. Project, feature, or even user story cost can be one of the biggest determiners of whether a company chooses to invest in development or not. Like it or not, we are going to need Cycle Time data to figure out development cost.

There is still a more important reason to understand Cycle Time. Cycle Time represents the amount of time it takes to get customer feedback. Customer feedback is of vital importance in our knowledge work world. Value itself is ultimately determined by the customer, which means your team is going to want to make sure it gets that value feedback as quickly as possible. The last thing you want is to develop something that the customer does not need—especially if it takes you forever to do so. Shortening Cycle Time will shorten the customer feedback loop. And to shorten Cycle Time, you are going to first need to measure it.

A final reason to monitor Cycle Time is that it can give you an overall picture of your process's health. The diagnostic tool needed for that is something called Flow Efficiency. Simply put, Flow Efficiency is the ratio of the total elapsed time that an item was actively worked on to the total elapsed time that it took for an item to complete (its total Cycle Time). There's a subtlety in this definition that bears some explanation. As an item is flowing through a process it is in either one of two states. It is either being actively worked on or it is not being actively worked on. Examples of an item not being actively worked on is it is blocked by some external dependency (team, vendor, etc.), or it is queuing waiting to be pulled. In both of those examples, an item is accumulating Cycle Time but no one is actively working on it. To get Flow Efficiency, you take the Total Cycle Time, subtract out inactive time and then divide that result by the Total Cycle Time.

It is not uncommon for teams just starting out with managing for flow to have Flow Efficiencies in the 15% range. Think about that for a second. If a user story took 20 days to complete and had a Flow Efficiency of 15% that means that it spent only 3 days having someone actively work on it and it spent 17 days in some type of inactive state. If a user story took only 3 active days of work yet had 17 days of inactivity built into its Cycle Time, where do you think you should focus your process improvement activities? It is probably going to be very hard to improve on that 3 days of active time, but my guess there are tons of opportunities to get that 17 day number down. Any reduction of inactive time will by definition improve overall Cycle Time. Looking at wait time is usually the best, easiest, cheapest area to investigate first for process improvement.

Throughput

I have saved the easiest metric to define for last. Simply put, Throughput is defined as:

 Throughput: the amount of WIP (number of work items) completed per unit of time.

Stated a slightly different way, Throughput is a measure of how fast items depart a process. The unit of time that your team chooses for your Throughput measurement is completely up to you. Your team can choose to measure the number of items that it gets done per day, per week, per iteration, etc. For example, you might state that the Throughput of your system as "three stories per day" (for a given day) or "five features per month" (for a given month).

A further thing to know about Throughput, however, is that this metric as I have defined it here is very different from the Scrum metric of "Velocity". Velocity, as you may know, is measured in terms of Story Points per sprint or iteration. You have to remember, though, that for Throughput I am talking about actual counts of work items (e.g., actual number of discrete stories and *not*

Story Points) per unit of time. As I have just mentioned, the unit of time you choose for Throughput is completely up to you. The implication being that your choice of a time period need not necessarily coincide with an iteration boundary. I say all of this because many agile coaches and consultants use the words "Velocity" and "Throughput" interchangeably. Just know that these two terms are definitely *not synonymous*.

If Throughput is how fast items depart from a process, then Arrival Rate is how fast items arrive to a process. I mention this fact here because depending on your perspective, Arrival Rate can be thought of as an analog to Throughput. For example, let's say that the "Development" step and "Test" step are adjacent in your workflow. Then the Throughput from the "Development" step could also be thought of as the Arrival Rate to the "Test" step.

Even more importantly, though, comparing the Arrival Rate of one step in your process to the Throughput in another, different step may give you some much needed insight into predictability problems. I will be going into much more detail about this comparison in the coming chapters. However, my more immediate reason in discussing Arrival Rate is simply to point out that how fast things arrive to your process could be just as important as how fast things depart.

The Throughput metric answers the very important question of "How many features am I going to get in the next release?" At some point you are going to need to answer that question, so track Throughput and be prepared.

As with the other metrics, though, the most obvious reason to track a metric is not necessarily the best reason to do so. While I am on record as being skeptical of applying the Theory of Constraints (ToC) to knowledge work, I will acknowledge that understanding Throughput at each step of your process will help you to identify the constraints in your workflow (assuming variability has been taken into account—but more on that later). Understanding what the constraints are and where they are will assist you in trying to determine (among other things) the best places to look for overall process improvement. Does your team require more staff? What type of staff do you need? Should you introduce some type of automation? These are all examples of questions that can only be answered by understanding and tracking Throughput.

Conclusion

What I have shown here are just the basic metrics of flow to get you started: WIP, Cycle Time, and Throughput. There are most certainly other metrics that you will want to track in your own environment, but these represent the metrics common to all flow implementations. If your goal is predictability, then these are the metrics that you are going to want to track.

I would also like to say one final word on vocabulary. No doubt if you have done any reading on this topic that you have come across different names for the concepts that I have defined in this chapter (I discussed the most contentious example of this in the "Lead Time vs. Cycle Time" section above). As I mentioned earlier, the point of this discussion is not to spark any religious wars over nomenclature. I am in no way trying to suggest that the names that I use here are the only correct ones. The point of this chapter is only to get you thinking about the basic concepts that are communicated by these metrics.

For example, for us to have a conversation about

predictability, we are first going to need some notion of the total amount of items in a system. I am choosing to call that notion Work In Progress. If you prefer the term Work in Process or something else, then by all means use that name. We are also going to need some notion of the amount of time that items spend in the system. I am choosing to call that Cycle Time. If you prefer Lead Time, Flow Time, Time In Process, or something else, then, please do not let me stand in your way. Lastly, we need some notion of the amount of items that leave the system per unit of time. I am choosing to call that Throughput. But please feel free to use the terms Completion Rate, Departure Rate, or anything else that you may make you comfortable (so long as you do not use the term Velocity!).

Just know that it is the definitions of these concepts that are important—not the names. However, to be clear, the rest of this book will utilize the names and definitions of these metrics as I have outlined in this chapter.

Lastly, one of the fundamental hypotheses of this chapter is that all processes can be modeled as queuing systems. When thinking about your process in this way, you are able to bring to bear the real reason why it is so crucial to track WIP, Cycle Time, and Throughput. This real reason is because these flow metrics are inextricably linked by a fundamental and powerful bond. Understanding this connection is going to be the key to building and operating a predictable process. An exploration of this link is where I will go next in my discussion of actionable metrics.

The name of this remarkable relationship, by the way, is Little's Law.

Key Learnings and Takeaways

- Any work item can be counted as WIP when it is between the defined entry point of a process and the defined exit point of a process.
- The choice of what work items you count as WIP when between those two points is completely up to you.
- WIP can be segmented into several different types.
- If WIP is segmented into several types, then it is also valid to talk about the Cycle Time and Throughput of those type segments.
- Cycle Time and Throughput are always defined in terms of WIP.
- Cycle Time is the amount of elapsed time that an item spends as Work In Progress.
- Throughput is the amount of Work In Progress completed during some arbitrary interval of time.
- The names of metrics are not as important as their definitions. Use whatever names you want for these metrics, but make sure you define them as they are defined here.
- Track these metrics because they have predictive power, are inexpensive to gather, and answer the important questions that your customers are asking.
- Track these metrics because they form the basis for Little's Law.

Chapter 3 - Introduction to Little's Law

The previous chapter dealt with the basic metrics of flow: WIP, Cycle Time, and Throughput. In what may be one of the most miraculous results in the history of process analysis, these three metrics are intrinsically linked by a very straightforward and very powerful relationship known as Little's Law:

 Average Cycle Time = Average Work In Progress / Average Throughput

If you have ever seen Little's Law before, you have probably seen it in the form of the above equation. What few Agile practitioners realize, however, is that Little's Law was originally stated in a slightly different form:

 Average Items In Queue = Average Arrival Rate * Average Wait Time

This fact is important because different assumptions need to be satisfied depending on which form of the law you are using. And understanding the assumptions behind the equation is the key to understanding the law itself. Once you understand the assumptions, then you can use those assumptions as a guide to some process policies that you can put in place to aid predictability.

The math of Little's Law is simple. But this chapter is about how we do not care about the math. What we do care about—and I cannot stress this point enough if we want to gain a greater appreciation of the law's applicability to our world—is looking far beyond the elegance of the equation to get a deeper understanding of the background assumptions needed to make the law work. That is where things get more complicated, but it is also where we will find the greatest benefit. A thorough comprehension of why Little's Law works the way it does is going to be the basis for understanding how the basic metrics of flow can become predictably actionable.

We Need a Little Help

First, some background.

Dr. John Little spent much of his early career studying queuing systems like Figure 2.1 (the queuing systems picture from the previous chapter). In fact, one of the best definitions of such a queuing system comes from Dr. Little himself: "A queuing system consists of discrete objects we shall call items, which arrive at some rate to the system. The items could be cars at a toll booth, people in a cafeteria line, aircraft on a production line, or instructions waiting to be executed inside a computer. The stream of arrivals enters the system, joins one or more queues and eventually receives service, and exits in a stream of departures. The service might be a taxi ride (travelers), a bowl of soup (lunch eaters), or auto repair (car owners). In most cases, service is the bottleneck that creates the queue, and so we usually have a service operation with a service time, but this is not required. In such a case we assume there is nevertheless a waiting time. Sometimes a distinction is made between number in queue and total number in queue plus service, the latter being called number in system." The diversity of domains that he mentions here is extraordinary. While he does not specifically mention software development or knowledge work in general, I am going to suggest that these areas can also be readily modeled in this way.

In 1961, Dr. Little set out to prove what seemed to be a very general and very common result exhibited by all queuing systems. The result that he was researching was a connection between the average Arrival Rate of a queue, the average number of items in the queue, and the average amount of time an item spent in the queue (for the purpose of this chapter, when I say "average" I am really talking about "arithmetic mean"). Mathematically, the relationship between these three metrics looks like:

 Equation (1): $L = \lambda * W$

Where:

L = the average number of items in the queuing system.

λ = the average number of items arriving per unit time.

W = the average wait time in the system for an item.

Notice that Equation (1) is stated strictly in terms of a queuing system's Arrival Rate. This point is going to be of special interest a little later in this chapter.

Also notice that—if it is not obvious already—Little's Law is a relationship of averages. Most knowledge work applications and discussions of the law neglect this very important detail. The fact that Little's Law is based on averages is not necessarily good or bad. It is only bad when people to try to apply the law for uses that it was never intended.

Dr. Little was the first to provide a rigorous proof for Equation (1) and, as such, this relationship has since been known as Little's Law. According to him, one of the reasons why the law is so important is the fact that (emphasis is mine): "L, λ, and W are three quite different and important measures of effectiveness of system performance, and Little's Law insists that they must obey the 'law.'... *Little's Law locks the three measures together in a unique and consistent way for any system in which it applies. Little's Law will not tell the managers how to handle trade-offs or provide innovations to improve their chosen measures, but it lays down a necessary relation.* As such, it provides structure for thinking about any operation that can be cast as a queue and suggests what data might be valuable to collect."

The great advantage of Little's Law is the overall simplicity of its calculation. Specifically, if one has any two of the above three statistics, then one can easily calculate the third. This result is extremely useful as there are many situations in many different domains where the measurement of all three metrics of interest is difficult, expensive, or even impossible. Little's Law shows us that if we can measure any two attributes, then we automatically get the third.

To illustrate this point, Dr. Little used the very simple example of a wine rack. Let's say you have a wine rack that, on average, always has 100 bottles in it. Let's further say that you replenish the rack at an average rate of two bottles per week. Knowing just these two numbers (and nothing else!) allows us to determine how long, on average, a given bottle spends sitting in the rack. By applying Equation (1), we have L equal to 100 and λ equal to 2. Plugging those numbers into the formula tells us that a given wine bottle spends, on average, 50 weeks in the rack.

Before we get much further, it is worth exploring what necessary contextual conditions are required for the law to hold. When stated in the form of Equation (1) the only assumption necessary is that the system under consideration has some guarantee of being in a steady state. That's it. Really, that's it. To illustrate the things we do not need, notice that we can arrive at the wine rack result without tracking the specific arrival or departure dates for each or any individual bottle. We also do not need to know the specific order that the bottles were placed in the rack, or the specific order that the bottles were taken off the rack. We do not need to understand anything fancy like the underlying probability distributions of the Arrival and Departure Rates. Interestingly, we do not even need to track the size of the bottles in the rack. We could have some small 20cl bottles or some large 2 litre bottles in addition to the more standard 750ml bottles. The variation in size has no impact on the basic result. (You should know that, in the interest of thoroughness, I am in the process of independently verifying this wine rack result on my own. Rest assured that no detail has been overlooked in the research of this book.)

As remarkable as all of this may be, the mathematics are not really what is important for our purposes here. What is important is that we acknowledge that the fundamental relationship exists. Understanding the inextricable link among these metrics is one of the most powerful tools at our disposal in terms of predictable process design.

But before we can get into how Little's Law can help us with predictability, it is probably helpful to first state the relationship in more familiar terms.

Little's Law from a Different Perspective

In the late 1980s (or early 1990s depending on whom you ask) Little's Law was usurped by the Operations Management (OM) community and was changed to emphasize OM's focus on Throughput. The OM crowd thus changed the terms in Little's Law to reflect their different perspective as shown by Equation (2):

 Equation (2): Cycle Time = Work In Progress / Throughput

Where:

1. **Cycle Time (CT)** = the average amount of time it takes for an item to flow through the system.
2. **Work In Progress (WIP)** = the average total inventory in the system.
3. **Throughput (TH)** = the average Throughput of the system.

In the interest of completeness, it is ok to perform the algebra on Little's Law so that it takes the different, yet still valid forms:

 Equation (3): TH = WIP / CT

and

 Equation (4): WIP = CT * TH

Where CT, WIP, and TH are defined the same way as in Equation (2).

Because of its roots in Operations Management, the Lean and Kanban knowledge work community has adopted this "Throughput" form of Little's Law as their own. If you have seen Little's Law before, you have almost certainly seen it in the form of Equation (2)—even though Equation (2) does not represent the law's original format.

The upshot of Little's Law is that, in general, the more things that you work on at any given time (on average) the longer it is going to take for each of those things to finish (on average). As a case in point, managers who are ignorant of this law panic when they see that their Cycle Times are too long and perform the exact opposite intervention of what they should do: they start more work. After all, they reason, if things take so long, then they need to start new items as soon as possible so that those items finish on time—regardless of what is currently in progress. The result is that items only take longer and longer to complete. Thus, managers feel more and more pressure to start things sooner and sooner. You can see how this vicious cycle gets started and perpetuates itself. After studying Little's Law, you should realize that if Cycle Times are too long then the first thing you should consider is lowering WIP. It feels uncomfortable, but it is true. In order to get stuff done faster, you need to work on less (again, on average).

What Dr. Little demonstrated is that the three flow metrics are all essentially three sides of the same coin (if a coin could have three sides). By changing one of them, you will almost certainly affect one or both of the other two. In other words, Little's Law reveals what levers that we can pull when undertaking process improvement. Further, as we are about to see, Little's Law will suggest the specific interventions that we should explore when our process is not performing the way we think it should.

At the risk of repeating myself, what I am talking about here is simple, incontrovertible mathematical fact. A change in one metric almost always results in a change in the others. Most companies that I talk to that complain of poor predictability are almost always ignorant of the negative implication of too much WIP on Cycle Time or Throughput. Ignore this correlation at your own peril.

It is all about the Assumptions

This is all straightforward enough so far, right? Well, unfortunately, it is not. Remember I said at the outset that Little's Law is deceptively simple? Here is where things get more complicated.

It is easy to see from a purely mathematical perspective that Equation (1) is logically equivalent to Equation (2). But it is more important to focus on the difference between the two. As I mentioned earlier, Equation (1) is expressly stated in terms of the *Arrival Rate* to the system whereas Equation (2) is expressly stated in terms of the *Departure Rate* from the system. This emphasis on Throughput in Equation (2) probably seems more comfortable to us as it reflects the usual perspective of a knowledge work process. Typically, in our context, we care about the rate at which we are finishing our work (even though, as we shall soon see, we should care just as much about the rate at which we start work). What is nice to know is that Little's Law can morph to match this required perspective.

At first glance, this change may not otherwise seem all that significant. However, this transformation from the perspective of arrivals to the perspective of departures has a profound impact in terms of how we think about and apply the law. When we state Little's Law in terms of a system's Throughput then we must also immediately consider what underlying assumptions must be in place in order for the departure-oriented law to be valid.

Earlier when I first introduced Equation (1) I had stated that there was really only one assumption that needed to be in place for it to work. Well, in the interest of completeness, technically there were three. For Equation (1) we need:

1. A steady state (i.e., that the underlying stochastic processes are stationary)
2. An arbitrarily long period of time under observation (to guarantee the stationarity of the underlying stochastic processes)
3. That the calculation be performed using consistent units (e.g., if wait time is stated in days, then Arrival Rate must also be stated in terms of days).

By the way, the point here is to not give you an advanced degree in statistics or queuing theory. Do not worry if you do not know what "stochastic" or "stationary" means. You do not need to. As I have just said, I mention these things for completeness only.

When we shift perspective to look at Little's Law from the perspective of Throughput rather than from the perspective of Arrival Rate, however, we also need to change the assumptions necessary for the law to be valid. This point is so important, I want to place it in its own callout:

Looking at Little's Law from the perspective of Throughput rather than from the perspective of Arrival Rate necessitates a change in the assumptions required for the law to be valid.

When applying the Throughput form of Little's Law (Equation (2)), there are two basic cases to consider. Each case is going to require its own assumption to be valid.

The first case is if the total amount of WIP in our process is ever allowed to go to zero. If so, then Little's Law is exact between any two time instances where total process WIP is zero. Yes, I did say exact. Further, only one additional assumption (other than a start and end with zero WIP) is needed for the law to work in this case. All we require is that everything that enters the system eventually exits. No other assumptions about stable systems or no other assumptions about the length of the time period. Nothing. Reflect on this result for second and see if you can think of any circumstance where you start a time period with zero WIP and end the time period with zero WIP. Two examples immediately come to my mind. An ideal software "project" would start with zero WIP and end with zero WIP. If that is the case, then at the end of the project, using Little's Law we could exactly determine the average of any of the three basic metrics of flow assuming we collected data on the other two. Another good example would be any Scrum sprint. If you are doing canonical Scrum, then, by definition you start each sprint with zero WIP and you end each sprint with zero WIP (remember, we are talking textbook Scrum here—I know practice usually falls far short of prescription). If so, then just as in the previous example, you could use Little's Law to calculate an average of any of the three basic metrics of flow assuming that you have collected the data for the other two.

Unfortunately, though, most of us do not live in a world where we ever run out of WIP. Some examples for this might be: we work on multiple projects at a time or there is never a clean break between when one project starts and another finishes, we are forced to do maintenance requests and production support in addition to project work, we never finish all the work that we had started at the beginning of sprints, etc.

Which brings us to the second case: when WIP never goes to zero. In this case we have to be much more careful about the assumptions that are required for a valid application of Little's Law.

When WIP never goes to zero, then the assumptions about our process that are necessary to make Little's Law (in the form of Equation (2)) work are:

1. The average input or Arrival Rate (λ) should equal the average output or Departure Rate (Throughput).
2. All work that is started will eventually be completed and exit the system.
3. The amount of WIP should be roughly the same at the beginning and at the end of the time interval chosen for the calculation.
4. The average age of the WIP is neither increasing nor decreasing.
5. Cycle Time, WIP, and Throughput must all be measured using consistent units.

As a quick aside, even if the assumptions do not hold for the entire time period under consideration, Little's Law can still be used as an estimation. However, the "goodness" of the estimation depends on how badly the assumptions have been violated.

The first two assumptions (#1 and #2) comprise a notion known as Conservation of Flow. I will spend a lot of time talking about this principle in Chapter 7 and Chapter 8. The second two assumptions (#3 and #4) speak to the notion of system stability. I will also spend a lot of time talking about one way to recognize unstable systems in Chapter 9.

The last assumption (#5) is necessary for the math (and any corresponding analysis) to come out correctly (you will notice this is the same assumption necessary when stating the law in terms of arrivals). The necessity for using consistent units when performing a Little's Law calculation should be intuitively obvious, but it is fairly easy to get tripped up over this. When we say "consistent" units what we are really saying is, for example, if we are measuring average Cycle Time using the unit of time "day", then the average Throughput must be in the form of the number of items per that same unit of time (day), and the average WIP must be the average amount of items for one unit of time (day). As another example, if you want to measure average Throughput in terms of items per week (i.e., the unit of time here is "week"), then average Cycle Time must be stated in terms of weeks, and average WIP must be the average for each week. - You might think I am wasting your time by mentioning this, but you would be surprised how many teams miss this point (one is immediately reminded of when NASA slammed an orbiter into the side of Mars because one team used metric units while another used English units—moral of the story: do not do that). For example, I saw one Scrum team that was measuring their velocity in terms of story points per sprint (as Scrum teams are wont to do). For their Little's

Law calculation, they proceeded to plug in their velocity number for Throughput, their WIP number as total number of user stories (actual stories—not story points) completed in the sprint, and expected to get a Cycle Time number in days. You can imagine their surprise when the numbers did not come out quite the way that they expected.

Assumptions as Process Policies

Understanding these foundational assumptions is of monumental importance. Despite what many people will tell you, the true power of Little's Law is not in performing the mathematical calculation by plugging numbers into its formula. Even though I have spent so much time on it already, I want you to forget about the arithmetic. In truth, most of us will never need to compute Little's Law. As I mentioned in the previous chapter, the three flow metrics' data is so easy to capture that you should never have to compute one of them—just go look at the data!

Rather, the true power of Little's Law lies in understanding the assumptions necessary for the law to work in the first place. If there are three things that I want you to have taken away from this conversation about Little's Law they are:

1. It is all about the assumptions.
2. It is all about the assumptions.
3. It is all about the assumptions.

Every time you violate an assumption of Little's Law your process becomes less predictable. Every time. This increased unpredictability may manifest itself as longer Cycle Times or more process variability or both. Or, worse still, these violations may not even immediately show up in your data. The whole time you are violating Little's Law your data may be showing you a rosier picture of the world than is really occurring. The danger here is that you may be basing some forecast on this overly optimistic view—only to find that things are much worse than they seemed.

Of course, we live in the real world and there are going to be times when violating these assumptions is going to be unavoidable or even necessary. But that is exactly why it is all the more important to understand the implications when these violations occur. There are always going to be things that happen to us that are outside of our control. However, the last thing we want to do is compound those uncontrollable events by allowing bad things to happen that were in our control and could have easily prevented. Control what you can control and then try to eliminate or mitigate the things you cannot.

The above principles (especially the first four) are going to help us do just that. We can use these assumptions as the basis for some simple policies that will govern the operation of our process. These policies will serve to control the things that we can control. These policies will serve to make our process more predictable.

Based on the assumptions above, some process policies might include (but certainly would not be limited to): - We will only start new work at about the same rate that we finish old work. - We will make every reasonable effort to finish all work that is started and minimize wasted effort due to discarded work items (this will necessitate some notion of late-binding "commitment"). - If work becomes blocked we will do everything we can do unblock that work as expeditiously as possible. - We will closely monitor our policies around the order in which we pull items through our system so that some work items do not sit and age unnecessarily.

The design of your process is really just the sum of all the policies you have in place. How well your system performs or does not perform is directly attributable to those policies and to how well you adhere or do not adhere to them. When I talk about designing for predictability, what I am talking about is giving you some clues—some insights—into appropriate policies that you can build into the day to day operation of your process. These policies will serve to normalize and stabilize your system in order to give your process the predictability that you are looking for. It is only from this stable base that we can even hope to implement real, long-lasting process improvement.

As my friend and colleague Frank Vega so often likes to say, "your policies shape your data and your data shape your policies". The policies that I have mentioned here will in no small way influence the data that you collect off of your process. That is a good thing, by the way. It is a good thing because that data in and of itself is potentially going to further suggest where our process policies are deficient. It is this virtuous cycle that I am talking about when I say "actionable metrics for predictability".

Segmenting WIP

I mentioned in Chapter 2 that it is possible to segment your WIP into several different types. For example it might be useful to think of your WIP not as just generic work items, but categorize it into types like "user stories", "production defects", "maintenance request", etc. This is a perfectly valid approach and actually may be desirable in most circumstances. The good news is that if you choose to segment your WIP in such a manner then Little's Law will apply to both the overall WIP in the system as well as to each type or groups of types.

For example, we might want to use Little's Law to analyze all work flowing through our system, or we may want to use it to just look at our work items that are of type "user story". We might want to investigate how badly our production defects are violating the assumptions of the law. Or maybe it is our maintenance requests grouped together with defects that are the culprit. In most cases this type of segmentation is very useful and could provide a more sophisticated approach to analyzing process performance.

For those of you thinking ahead and for those of you familiar with Kanban systems, you will notice that I have purposefully not used the term "Class of Service" here. Not to spoil the punchline, but, yes, you can use Little's Law if you choose to segment your WIP along different Classes of Service. This tactic has a particular significance when it comes to process predictability (spoiler alert: it is usually bad) which is why I have devoted a whole chapter (Chapter 13) to Class of Service later.

Kanban Systems

From a WIP perspective, it may seem that running a Kanban system guarantees Little's Law's assumptions are taken care of. There are several reasons why that may not be the case:

1. It is possible that changing WIP limits may have no effect on total average WIP (e.g., decreasing or increasing a WIP limit after a clear systemic bottleneck). This may be one reason you do not get the "forecasted" behavior you might expect from Little's Law.

2. Setting a WIP limit is not necessarily the same as limiting Work In Progress. I cannot tell you how many teams I come across that set WIP Limits but then routinely violate them. And violate them egregiously.
3. Average WIP over a time period is highly dependent on pull policies in place. E.g., are as many items as possible pulled in order to satisfy WIP limits at all times?

The point here is that if you are using a Kanban system, you cannot just simply add up all the WIP Limits on your board and think that you have calculated WIP for your process (as discussed previously in Chapter 2). You are going to have actually track physical WIP. Fortunately, I am going to show you a very easy way to do that in the next chapter!

Lastly, most people think that Little's Law is the single greatest reason to implement a Kanban-style Agile process. While I would not strictly disagree with that statement, I would offer a better way of stating it. I would say that Little's Law is the single greatest reason to move to a more WIP-limited, pull-based, continuous flow process. The thing is, once we do that, we can then start to use Little's Law as our guide for process predictability.

Size Does Not Matter

I have one last topic I want to cover before wrapping up. Notice how in the assumptions for Little's Law I made no mention a requirement for all work items to be of the same size. That is because no such requirement exists. Most people assume that an application of Little's Law specifically—and limiting WIP in general—necessitates that all work items be of the same size. That is simply not true. The precise reasons why would fill up a chapter in its own right, so I am going to limit my comments to two brief points.

First, work items size does not matter because for Little's Law we are dealing with relationships among averages. We do not necessarily care about each item individually, we care about what all items look like on average.

Second, and more importantly, the variability in work item size is probably not the variability that is killing your predictability. Your bigger predictability problems are usually too much WIP, the frequency with which you violate Little's Law's assumptions, etc. Generally those are easier problems to fix than trying to arbitrarily make all work items the same size. Even if you were in a context where size did matter, it would be more about right-sizing your work and not same-sizing your work (but more on that in Chapter 12).

Forecasting

As this is a book about predictability, my guess is that you were expecting me to say that once you understand Little's Law all you need to do is to plug in the numbers and out will pop the forecasting result that you are looking for (à la Newton's $F = ma$ or Einstein's $E=mc^2$). However, nothing could be further from the truth.

The first thing that you need to know about Little's Law is that it is concerned with looking backward over a time period that has completed. It is not about looking forward; that is, is not meant to be used to make *deterministic* predictions. As Dr. Little himself says about the law, "This is not all bad. It just says that we are in the measurement business, not the forecasting business".

This point requires a little more discussion as it is usually where people get hung up. The "law" part of Little's Law specifies an exact relationship between average WIP, average Cycle Time, and average Throughput, and this "law" part only applies only when you are looking back over historical data. The law is not about—and was never designed for—making deterministic forecasts about the future. For example, let's assume a team that historically has had an average WIP of 20 work items, an average Cycle Time of 5 days, and an average Throughput of 4 items per day. You cannot say that you are going to increase average WIP to 40, keep average Cycle Time constant at 5 days and magically Throughput will increase to 8 items per day—even if you add staff to the keep the WIP to staff ratio the same in the two instances. You cannot assume that Little's Law will make that prediction. It will not. All Little's Law will say is that an increase in average WIP will result in a change to one or both of average Cycle Time and average Throughput. It will further say that those changes will manifest themselves in ways such that the relationship among all three metrics will still obey that law. But what it does not say is that you can deterministically predict what those changes will be. You have to wait until the end of the time interval you are interested in and look back to apply the law.

But that restriction is not fatal. The proper application of Little's Law in our world is to understand the assumptions of the law and to develop process policies that match those assumptions. If the process we operate conforms—or mostly conforms—to all of the assumptions of the law then we get to a world where we can start to trust the data that we are collecting off of our system. It is at this point that our process is probabilistically predictable. Once there we can start to use something like Monte Carlo simulation on our historical data to make forecasts and, more importantly, we can have some confidence in the results we get by using that method.

There are other, more fundamental reasons why you do not want to use Little's Law to make forecasts. For one thing, I have hopefully by now beaten home the point that Little's Law is a relationship of averages. I mention this again because even if you could use Little's Law as a forecasting tool (which you cannot), you would not want to as you would be producing a forecast based on averages. There are all kinds of reasons why you should not forecast based on averages—too many to go into here. It turns out we can do better than averages, anyway, when collecting metrics data and there are going to be much better tools at our disposal when we are ready to do forecasting. Luckily for you, I will discuss some of those tools in Chapter 14 and Chapter 15 (I have just mentioned one of them in the previous paragraph).

Having said all that, though, there is no reason why you cannot use the law for quick, back-of-the-envelope type estimations about the future. Of course you can do that. I would not, however, make any commitments, staff hiring or firing decisions, or project cost calculations based on this type of calculation alone. I would further say that it is negligent for someone to even suggest to do so. But this simple computation might be useful as a quick gut-check to decide if something like a project is worth any further exploration.

Remember that being predictable is not completely about making forecasts. The bigger part of predictability is operating a system that behaves in a way that we expect it to. By designing and operating a system that follows the assumptions set forth by the Little's Law, we will get just that: a process that behaves the way we expect it to. That means we will have controlled the things that we can control and that the interventions that we take to make things better will result in outcomes more closely aligned with our expectations.

Conclusion

I know I have said it before, but I need to say it again: Little's Law is not about understanding the mathematics of queuing theory. It is about understanding the assumptions that need to be in place in order for the law to work. We can use those assumptions as a guide, or blueprint, or model for our own process policies. Whenever your process policies are in violation of the assumptions of Little's Law then you know that you have at least diminished—or possibly eliminated—your chance of being predictable.

As you operate your process think about the times and reasons why work flows in at a faster rate than work flows out. Think about why items age unnecessarily due to blockages or poor pull policies. Think about why work is abandoned when only partially complete (and how you account for that abandonment). Think about how these occurrences are violating the assumptions Little's Law and how they are ultimately affecting your ability to be predictable. But more importantly, think about how your understanding of Little's Law should result in behavior changes for you and your team. When violations of Little's Law occur, it is usually because of something you did or chose (intentionally or not) not to do. Remember, you have much more control over your process than you think you do.

Now that we have an understanding of Little's Law

and the basic metrics of flow, it is time to turn our attention to how these concepts are visualized through the use of flow analytics. As we are about to see, it is the quantitative and qualitative interpretation of these unique analytics that will make our process truly predictable, and will make the flow metrics truly actionable.

Key Learnings and Takeaways

- Little's Law relates the basic metrics of flow in an elegant, fundamental equation.
- Little's Law is a relationship of averages.
- Do not get distracted with the math of Little's Law—the significance of the law does not necessarily come from plugging numbers into the equation.
- When stating it in terms of Equation #2, for contexts with continuous WIP, there are five assumptions necessary for Little's Law to work, they are:
  - The average input or Arrival Rate (λ) should equal the average Throughput (Departure Rate).
  - All work that is started will eventually be completed and exit the system.
  - The amount of WIP should be roughly the same at the beginning and at the end of the time interval chosen for the calculation.
  - The average age of the WIP is neither increasing nor decreasing.
  - Cycle Time, WIP, and Throughput must all be measured using consistent units.
- Use these assumptions as a guide for your process policies. The more you violate these assumptions, the less chance you have of being predictable.

- Even if the assumptions do not hold for the entire time period under consideration, Little's Law can still be used as an estimation. However, the "goodness" of the estimation depends on how badly the assumptions have been violated.
- Little's Law is not for forecasting. To do forecasting we will need other tools. If someone tells you that you can forecast with Little's Law or shows you an example of how to do it, you have my permission to slap them (I put that in to see if you were still reading).
- If you segment your WIP into different types, then Little's Law can be applied to each of the different type segments.

PART TWO - CUMULATIVE FLOW DIAGRAMS FOR PREDICTABILITY

Chapter 4 - Introduction to CFDs

Over the next three chapters I will go into a fair amount of detail about what a Cumulative Flow Diagram (CFD) is, what information it can provide, and how to interpret the results. You might be tempted to skip this section if you believe you are already familiar with CFDs. I would ask that you do not. I say this because much of what has been published about CFDs' application to knowledge work is at best misleading and at worst completely wrong. This chapter aims to clear up some of the prevailing myths and misconceptions about these truly incredible charts. In order to clear up these myths, I need to introduce CFDs much differently than they are normally presented. My hope is to arm you with information you need to take full advantage of one of the most effective analytic tools at your disposal.

What makes a CFD a CFD?

The very first thing to know about Cumulative Flow Diagrams is that they are all about arrivals and departures. In fact, when researching this book, the very first reference that I could find to a CFD appeared in the 1960s and that article actually labeled the chart as a "Cumulative Arrival and Departures Diagram". I am not entirely sure when the name got changed to Cumulative Flow Diagram. However, as I have demonstrated in the previous chapters, the concepts of arrivals and departures are central to the idea of flow, so the name change makes perfect sense.

As its name suggests, therefore, a Cumulative Flow Diagram is an excellent way to visualize the flow of work through a process. CFDs are among the least known, and therefore one of the least understood charts in all of Agile analytics; yet, they represent one of the most powerful process performance gauges available to us. They are a powerful tool for a couple of reasons. First, these charts offer a concise, coherent visualization of the three metrics of flow that I introduced in Chapter 2. Second, they offer massive amounts of information at just a glance, or by just doing some very simple calculations. Visualizing flow via a CFD gives us both quantitative and qualitative insight into problems—or potential problems—in our process. Gaining an understanding of actual process performance is one of the necessary first steps for introducing overall system predictability.

In order to gain this insight, however, we have to be very precise in terms how we define exactly what a CFD is, and—more importantly—how to construct one. In a point that I will hammer over and over in this and the next two chapters, an improperly constructed CFD can lead to improper conclusions about process problems. Worse, improperly constructed CFDs can lead to team or management apathy amid claims that the charts are just not very useful.

So, without any further ado, let's get to it.

If you have never seen a Cumulative Flow Diagram before, then here is your chance:

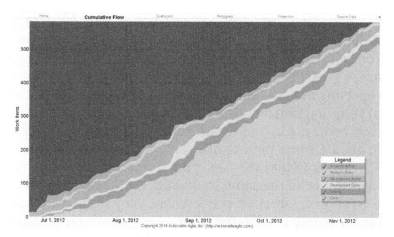

Figure 4.1: A Basic CFD

It may not look like much to you right now, but as I just mentioned this chart is actually communicating a lot of information.

To get you oriented with what you are looking at, I first want to spend some time going over the anatomy of a CFD. Once you have got that under your belt, then we can move on to what this graph is actually telling us.

The first thing to note about a CFD is that across the bottom (the X-axis) is some representation of a progression of time (usually calendar time). It could be said that the X-axis represents a timeline for our process. The tick marks on the X-axis represents our choice of labels for that timeline. When labeling the X-axis, you can choose whatever frequency of labels you want. In this particular CFD, we have chosen to label every month. However you can choose whatever label is best for your specific needs. You can choose to label every two weeks, every month, every day, etc.

A very important point here is that these labels can be very different than the reporting interval that you choose to build your CFD. The reporting interval is the frequency that you choose to add data to your chart. Just as with the labels, your reporting interval is up to you. You can choose to report on your process data every day, every week, every month, etc. Just note that whatever reporting interval that you choose will change the shape of your diagram (choosing a different reporting interval may certainly be the tweak you want to make in order to get a clearer picture of what's going on in the CFD). Further note that the reporting interval and the labels need not be of the same frequency. On the above graph, the reporting interval is every day, yet you can see that we have only labeled the timeline at every month.

Lastly, I should point out that in Figure 4.1 I have chosen to show the timeline progression from left to right. This is not a requirement, it is only a preference. I could have easily shown time progression from right to left. The vast majority of CFDs that you will come across (unless your name is Frank), however, will show the progression of time from left to right. Thus, for the rest of this chapter (and this book), I will show all CFD time progressions from left to right. Further, know that all properties of CFDs that I am about to describe assume a CFD with a time progression from left to right.

If across the bottom is a progression of time, then up the side (the Y-axis) is a cumulative count of items in the process. To build our CFD, at each reporting interval we are going to calculate the total number of items at each step in our process and plot them on our graph (how to properly "count" items will be explained a little later in this chapter). Just as with labels and reporting intervals, you can choose whatever scale you want for the work item axis. Choosing different scales will cause the picture to change, but, again, that may just be the adjustment you need in order to "sharpen" your chart's picture.

As you plot items at each reporting interval, then over time "bands" will emerge on your chart. Those bands will correspond to each of the workflow steps in your process, as in in Figure 4.2.

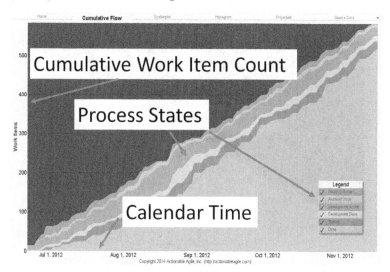

Figure 4.2: Anatomy of a CFD

A quick note about what I mean by "bands" on a CFD versus what I mean by "lines" on a CFD. By "band" I mean each different colored section on the graph. By "line" I mean the demarcation boundary of any band. Any band on a CFD is always going to be bounded by two lines: a top line and a bottom line. The bottom line of a given band will be the same as the top line of the succeeding band—should such a subsequent band exist. The chart in Figure 4.2, for example, has six bands corresponding to each of the process states and it has seven lines that mark the boundaries. For clarification, technically, the bottom line of the "Done" band in Figure 4.2 is the line that runs along the bottom of the chart at the X-axis. For the purposes of CFD definition, though, this line can be ignored.

Note: unless otherwise specified, when I say "top line of a CFD" I mean the top line of the top-most band. When I say "bottom line of a CFD" I mean the top line of the bottom-most band. This is illustrated in Figure 4.3:

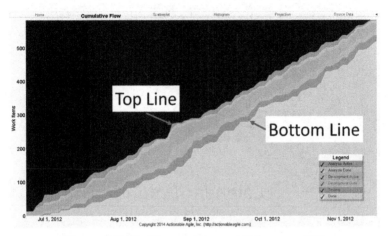

Figure 4.3: The Top and Bottom Line on a CFD

I began this section by pointing out that the most important thing to remember about CFDs is that they are fundamentally about process arrivals and departures. Any chart that does not model or graph these arrivals and departures properly or any chart that includes extraneous information not considered an arrival or departure cannot be properly called a Cumulative Flow Diagram. This brings us to the first of several fundamental properties of CFDs:

 CFD Property #1: The top line of a Cumulative Flow Diagram *always* represents the cumulative arrivals to a process. The bottom line on a CFD *always* represents the cumulative departures from a process.

When I say "always" I mean "always". Any chart that contains additional outside lines that do not represent process arrivals and departures is not a CFD. Also note the use of the word "cumulative" (this is a *Cumulative Flow Diagram*, after all). Any chart that does not account for cumulative arrivals and departures properly is not a CFD (more on this later). It is important to remember— as mentioned in Chapter 2—that the definition of the boundaries of your process is essentially up to you. However, once chosen, those boundaries will be represented by the lines on your graph as defined above. You can have as many bands that represent as many workflow steps as you want in between your two boundaries. As we will see, it can be very advantageous and strongly recommended—but by no means necessary—to represent those additional states on your diagram. If you do choose to include those additional states, then the top and bottom line of the band at each workflow step represents that state's arrivals and departures, respectively.

For example, let's say I have a process that looks like:

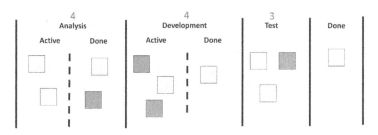

Figure 4.4: Example Process

Those of you familiar with Kanban may recognize this as a Kanban board, but the following discussion is equally applicable to a more Scrum or XP style of process that has columns as simple as "To Do", "Doing", and "Done" (how Kanban can be used to model a Scrum or XP process is well beyond the scope of this book; however, the principles discussed here apply regardless of the particular methodology that has been chosen).

In this example, arrivals to the process are denoted by the "Analysis Active" column, and departures from the process are denoted by the "Done" column. A simple CFD that models *only* the overall cumulative arrivals and departures in this process might look like:

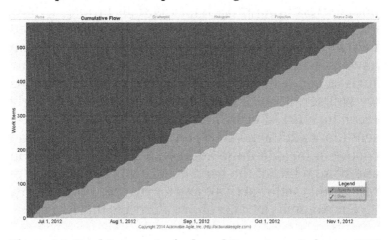

Figure 4.5: Total Process Arrivals and Departures Only on a CFD

Notice that there are only two bands on this diagram. As always, the top line of the top band represents the cumulative arrivals to the "Analysis" column and the top line of the bottom band represents the cumulative departures to the "Done" column. Figure 4.5 is a perfectly valid CFD for the process shown in Figure 4.4. One question that you may want to keep in the back of your mind as you go through this discussion is: what do you think the advantages or disadvantages of visualizing your flow as only two lines and bands as shown in Figure 4.5?

If we wanted a little more detail about our process,

we could easily include in the above diagram the cumulative arrivals and departures for each of the intermediate workflow steps between "Analysis Active" and "Done". If we were interested in doing so, then our CFD would morph into the diagram depicted in Figure 4.6:

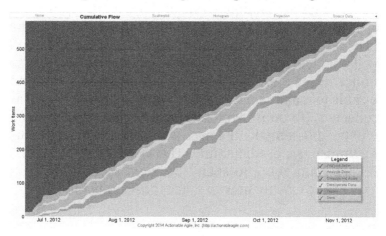

Figure 4.6: A Basic CFD

The several lines in Figure 4.6 now correspond to the cumulative arrivals and departures at each step in the workflow.

One quick thing before I proceed: you will notice that in this picture I have shown the queuing states or "Done" columns for Analysis and Development rather than just showing the Analysis and Development steps each as their own layer on the CFD. I have become a big fan of this approach as I believe this has the potential to give us greater insight into flow problems. For example, in the above chart we will potentially want to pay particular attention to the bands that represent the "Analysis Done" and "Development Done" columns. A widening of these layers could hint at something going wrong in our process—but I am getting a little ahead of myself here.

The final thing to know about CFDs is they are intrinsically linked with Little's Law. In fact, Dr. Little has used CFDs in several of his publications when explaining his eponymous law. I spent so much time in the last chapter discussing Little's Law's assumptions because many times a violation of one of those assumptions will clearly show up on a CFD. That is the good news. The bad news is that many times an assumption violation will not clearly reveal itself on a CFD. This is why it is so important to know the assumptions behind the law and be able to map them to the context in which the data was collected. If you understand the assumptions then you will be able to make the necessary process adjustments for improved predictability. The last bit of good news is that I am going to spend the next several chapters explaining exactly how to make those adjustments.

Constructing a CFD

The next step in learning how a CFD can help us is to understand how to construct one. To start, most people will tell you that to create a CFD, all you need to do is physically count all work items in progress at each step of your process and then just plot those counts on your chart at regular reporting intervals. I call this approach "building a chart based on counts". Not to put too fine a point on it, but building a chart just by counting items in progress is, in a word, dubious.

To explain why, I would like to explore an example that might illustrate the point better. For this example, I am going to use the same metaphor that Dr. Little himself has used in several of his publications.

Suppose that the system we wish to model is that of a supermarket. This particular shop may have set hours that it opens and closes each day, or it may be—as is the case with more and more American shops—open twenty-four hours a day and seven days a week. At various times throughout its hours of operation, it will have customers who enter and leave the shop. Some customers will make purchases while others will leave empty-handed.

Having this image in mind, let's explore two very important facts about our shop example:

1. Given its physical structure, it is very obvious to determine when customers have entered the shop and when customers have left the shop. Another way of saying this is that our shop has a very clear point at which customers are said to have arrived to the shop, and there is a very clear point at which customers are said to have departed the shop.
2. Every customer who enters the shop ultimately departs the shop. There are no customers who magically disappear. Even in the case of the continuously open shop, customers must inevitably and eventually leave. This fact is true regardless of how long customers spend in the shop or regardless of whether they made a purchase or not.

Going forward, let's assume we are dealing with a shop that is continuously open and that we are tracking hourly arrivals and departures (the "open-close" scenario will be discussed later).

In this example, how might we visualize the flow of customers on a CFD? Well, as I have just stated, a CFD is all about arrivals and departures, so the first thing we need to ask ourselves: how do we determine if someone has arrived or departed our shop? One of the reasons I chose this particular example is because answering that question in this scenario is actually very easy. An arriving customer is anyone who enters the shop from the outside, and a departing customer is anyone who leaves the shop from the inside. To calculate these arrivals and departures, we could easily install turnstiles at all doors and count the number of people who enter and exit over time. These turnstiles would not track how long each individual spent in the shop, nor would they be able to tell us if a departing individual made a purchase or not. They would, however, increment an arrival count for each customer who entered the shop (went from the outside in) and increment a departure's count for each customer who exited (went from the inside out). Every hour we could go and read those counts off the turnstiles and plot them our graph. If we were tracking those counts in a spreadsheet, the data might look like Figure 4.7:

Hour	Entered Shop	Exited Shop
8:00	11	0
9:00	24	8
10:00	30	15
11:00	31	23
12:00	57	31
13:00	66	48
14:00	74	62
15:00	80	69
16:00	95	71

Figure 4.7: Cumulative Count of Arrivals and Departures for the Shop Example

If using a spreadsheet, this data could easily be converted into an Area Chart. That Area Chart, in this case, would be a CFD. Using the data from above, our Cumulative Flow Diagram for this example might look like Figure 4.8:

Figure 4.8: Excel CFD for Shop Example

Let's say now that we want to add a process step that is "checkout". Let's further say our shop has a single queue that feeds all cashiers. We could then install one turnstile that all customers go through to get to the checkout queue and count arrivals as before. Additionally, let's say that after completing their purchase, all customers must exit the shop through the overall shop departures turnstile. Our data might now look like Figure 4.9:

Hour	Entered Shop	Checkout	Exited Shop
8:00	11	1	0
9:00	24	12	8
10:00	30	19	15
11:00	31	26	23
12:00	57	42	31
13:00	66	53	48
14:00	74	67	62
15:00	80	76	69
16:00	95	88	71

Figure 4.9: Adding a Checkout Step to the Shop Example

And our CFD would now look like Figure 4.10:

Figure 4.10: Adding Checkout Line to Shop CFD in Excel

This example is straightforward enough so far, but it gets very tricky when we start consider some special cases. For instance, how do we account for those customers who enter the shop but then immediately turn around and leave for any number of reasons: maybe they forgot their shopping list, maybe they got a call and need to go outside for better reception or privacy, etc.? Do we really want to count those customers as having "arrived" and "departed" the shop? Maybe. Maybe not. Similarly, what about those customers who enter the checkout queue but leave immediately because they realize that they failed to pick up an item, because they picked up the wrong items, or because they decide that they do not want to make any purchase after all? Do we really want to count those customers as having "arrived" and "departed" the checkout queue?

The skeptics out there might be thinking that the answer to this problem is easy. In these special cases, simply decrement the arrival count. However, if this decrementing of arrival count happens across the reporting interval, the net effect is that the lines on our CFD will go down. That is to say, if our reporting interval is every hour on the hour, and four customers arrive at 9:59am (and we increment our arrival count), but they then leave at 10:01am for one of the special cases above (and we decide to decrement our arrival count) then the data in our spreadsheet will look like Figure 4.11:

Hour	Entered Shop	Checkout	Exited Shop
8:00	11	1	0
9:00	24	12	8
10:00	30	19	15
11:00	27	26	23
12:00	57	42	31
13:00	66	53	48
14:00	74	67	62
15:00	80	76	69
16:00	95	88	71

Figure 4.11: Data for Non-Standard Departures

And our CFD will look like Figure 4.12:

Figure 4.12: Excel CFD for Non-Standard Departures

The difference between Figure 4.9 and Figure 4.11 is subtle but important. Note that the "Entered Shop" line in Figure 4.11 actually goes down. You might be thinking "No problem. We have modeled exactly what happened." But did we? I would argue that we did not. That customer physically arrived to our shop and then left. If we first increment then subsequently decrement our arrival count then we have a possibility of a negative arrival rate (which, by the way, violates the whole principle of a *Cumulative* Flow Diagram). But in the real world it is not possible to have a negative arrival rate. Arrivals are binary: either something has arrived or it has not. To handle the case of a non-standard departure, we essentially have two choices: (1) count a customer as having arrived and then departed; or (2) not count a customer as having arrived at all—i.e., it was a mistake to ever have incremented our arrival count in the first place.

This is where building a CFD based on counts breaks down and why it is very difficult—and not at all recommended—

to build a CFD just by counting items.

So if we cannot use counts, what do we use to create a CFD? The best approach would be to give each individual customer a timestamp for when they entered the shop, for when they entered the checkout queue, and for when they departed the shop. An example of this data might be what is shown in Figure 4.13:

Customer ID	Entered Shop	Checkout	Exited Shop
5	8:10	9:12	9:19
6	8:17	8:34	8:58
7	8:18		8:19
8	8:22	8:33	
9	9:01		

Figure 4.13: Timestamps for Customers

If a customer now exits the shop for any reason other than a "normal" one then we could reflect that in our data in one of two ways. First, we could choose to enter a departure timestamp and then "tag" that departure with a special reason. This would give us an opportunity to filter out that "bad" data if we choose to do so when building our CFD (this tag and filter strategy could be employed for other work item types as well, but more on that later). This particular approach is potentially best for customers who leave a queue and we do not expect them to return. A spreadsheet that shows this approach might look like Figure 4.14:

Customer ID	Entered Shop	Checkout	Exited Shop	Exception
5	8:10	9:12	9:19	
6	8:17	8:34	8:58	
7	8:18		8:19	Went to wrong shop
8	8:22	8:33		
9	9:01			

Figure 4.14: "Tagging" a customer with an Exception Reason

Second, we could choose to simply delete the arrival

timestamp as if the customer never entered the particular downstream queue. This strategy would be an acknowledgement that it was a mistake to ever have counted the arrival in the first place. This case might be a better solution for items that we expect to return to the queue at a later date (e.g., the situation where a customer leaves the checkout queue to go pick up additional items but who will ultimately return to checkout).

When building a proper CFD, either of these approaches is valid. This brings us to the second fundamental principle of CFDs:

 CFD Property #2: Due to its cumulative nature, no line on a CFD can ever decrease (go down).

You can immediately spot that a CFD has not been constructed properly if you see lines on the chart that go down. A properly constructed CFD always has lines that are either increasing (going up) or are flat. Not to belabor the point, but this non-decreasing effect is precisely why these charts are called *Cumulative* Flow Diagrams.

I hope you see how this example very closely parallels the types of decisions that we make every day in our knowledge work process. A customer who enters a shop but then abruptly leaves is akin to an item that arrives to the Analysis Active column of the board shown in Figure 4.4 but then gets taken off the board for whatever reason (de-prioritized, de-scoped, etc.). In this case it might be best to simply remove the timestamp that had been given to the item when it was placed in the Analysis Active column and proceed as if it had never arrived.

A customer who enters the checkout queue but then leaves for whatever reason is akin to an item that has made it to the Test column in Figure 4.3, but then it is determined the item should not be in Test. If the reason it should not be in test is because it is so broken that it cannot even be tested, then the item should be moved back to an appropriate prior step (Development, Analysis, etc.) and the timestamp for the Test column should be erased. If the item should not be in Test because it is determined that the item is no longer needed, then it should be moved directly to Done, given a departure timestamp and potentially flagged as—for example— "no longer needed". (By the way, the normal discovery of defects in the test column, to me, does not normally constitute an egregious enough offense to cause the item to be moved back to the development column.)

Thus, in knowledge work, in order to properly construct a CFD, what we really need to do is track the date that a particular item enters each step of our work flow. An example of what that data might look like is shown in Figure 4.15:

Story_ID	Analysis Active	Analysis Done	Development Active	Development Done	Testing	Done
1	06/25/2012	06/25/2012	06/26/2012	06/28/2012	06/29/2012	06/29/2012
2	06/25/2012	06/25/2012	06/27/2012	06/29/2012	06/29/2012	06/29/2012
3	06/21/2012	06/21/2012	06/21/2012	06/27/2012	06/27/2012	07/02/2012
4	06/21/2012	06/21/2012	06/21/2012	06/27/2012	06/27/2012	07/02/2012
5	06/21/2012	06/21/2012	06/21/2012	06/28/2012	07/02/2012	07/02/2012
6	06/21/2012	06/22/2012	06/22/2012	06/28/2012	06/28/2012	07/02/2012
7	06/25/2012	06/25/2012	06/25/2012	06/26/2012	06/29/2012	07/02/2012
8	06/25/2012	06/25/2012	06/25/2012	06/26/2012	06/29/2012	07/02/2012
9	06/21/2012	06/22/2012	06/22/2012	06/28/2012	06/28/2012	07/03/2012
10	06/25/2012	07/02/2012	07/02/2012	07/05/2012	07/06/2012	07/06/2012

Figure 4.15: Example Data for building a CFD

As mentioned previously, it is rather straight forward to turn this data into a format we can use to build a CFD. The added bonus of using this format is that by collecting dates this way, we now have all the data we will need to calculate all the metrics and analytics to be discussed in the rest of this book. I cannot stress this particular point enough: by collecting data in this way, not only are we assured of being able to build a correct CFD, but we also get all the data we need to build an array of other very useful charts—i.e., the analytics we need to help us along the path toward predictability.

I have mentioned several times now that you should not create a CFD from counting work items in progress at each step in your workflow at every reporting interval. Why do I make that statement when probably every other reference you have read about CFDs says that you should create your charts from item counts?

The only time you can use counts to create a CFD is if your data satisfies both of the following conditions:

1. You never have items that move backward in your workflow
2. You never have items that are just completely removed from your process before they are completed (presumably never to be heard from again)

I do not know about you, but I happen to live in the real world and in every process I have ever been a part of, I have had at least one—if not both—of these things happen and usually on multiple occasions.

Let's take point #2 first. I hope it is easy to imagine that if all you are doing is tracking counts, and items are simply removed from the process (by any other means than going to your Done state) then it is quite possible to have lines that go down (decrease) on your CFD. This situation quite obviously violates CFD Property #2. You could easily remedy this problem by making sure that every item that exits the process gets counted as part of the items in your "Done" state. This solution is perfectly legitimate and, further, I would recommend you do this regardless of how you collect your data (it might be further beneficial to tag these items that do not complete "correctly" with some metadata).

Which brings us to point #1. If you will remember, this is exactly the situation that I outlined in the shop metaphor section, so I will refer you to that section for the more detailed discussion of backward flow. Very quickly, though, remember that items that move backward—if not accounted for properly—can cause the lines on our CFD to go down, which, again, violates Property #2 of CFDs.

Lastly, and I really cannot stress this point enough, to do any more serious analysis of your flow, you are going to need to capture date data as opposed to counts anyway (to measure things like Cycle Time and to build some of the other analytics that we will discuss in later chapters). So since you can create a CFD from dates, why not just use those?

Another thing that you have probably noticed by now that none of the CFD examples I have shown have a line labelled "backlog". There are some very good reasons for that. For example, why cannot I have a picture that looks like Figure 4.16:

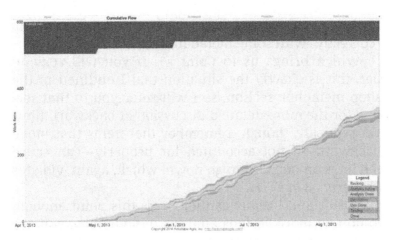

Figure 4.16: Showing a Backlog on a Chart

For the most part, any diagram that shows a backlog is not a CFD. To explain why, I would first like to describe my problem with the word "backlog" itself.

I am not trying to denigrate any particular process here, but, unfortunately, the word backlog is so prevalent nowadays that its use carries with it connotations that are counter-productive. Whether or not those connotations are correct is a different debate; the point here is to just acknowledge that they exist.

It has been my experience that people immediately assume two things when using the term backlog:

1. That items placed in a backlog are somehow committed to (or that they otherwise inherently have value), and,
2. That items placed in a backlog are somehow prioritized.

A backlog, therefore, is merely a convenient container for these candidate ideas. Commitment does not happen until a team actually has capacity, and prioritization does not happen until at the time of commitment (see Chapter 8 for how just-in-time commitment and prioritization work).

To be clear, you could definitely have a CFD that looks like Figure 4.16, but then it would be subject to all the properties of a CFD that I have outlined in this chapter. If you do not want to signal that items in your backlog have been committed to, then do not include a backlog band on your chart. If you do want communicate that backlog items have been committed to, then, by all means, display the backlog. That decision, as we are about to see, could have serious ramifications for your Cycle Time calculation.

I am not saying that a chart that shows a backlog is not useful—far from it. However, for the most part, a diagram that has a backlog on it is not a CFD. But, you may ask, "How then are we to do projections of when we will be done?" First, if you would like to do projections on a graph, then what you want is a something other than a CFD. Second, if you are truly serious about projections, then what you really should be doing is some type of probabilistic modeling like Monte-Carlo simulation. Projections, Burn-Ups, Release Planning, and Monte-Carlo simulation will all be covered in Chapter 14 and Chapter 15.

Conclusion

Mapping cumulative arrivals and departures to a process over time is one of the best tools you have at your disposal to visualize flow. Observing flow in this way allows us to discern an impressive amount of useful information regarding the health of our process.

To suitably construct a CFD, therefore, we must account for arrivals and departures appropriately. One

of the best ways to ensure that arrivals and departures
are displayed correctly is to make sure that we capture
the date that items enter each step of our workflow (as
illustrated in Figure 4.14). Those dates can then easily
and accurately be converted into the data we need to
build a proper CFD.

Now that you know what CFDs are all about and how
to construct them, it is time to get on to understanding
what these graphs are telling us.

Key Learnings and Takeaways

- CFDs demonstrate the cumulative arrivals and de-
  partures to a process over time, and, as such, are
  one of the best tools available for visualizing flow.
- This type of visualization communicates a lot of
  quantitative and qualitative information at a glance.
- The anatomy of a CFD is:
  - The X-axis represents the process timeline.
  - The Y-axis represents the cumulative count of
    items in the process at each reporting interval.
  - The labels and reporting intervals on the chart
    are at the sole discretion of the graph's cre-
    ator.
- Understanding the correct way to construct a CFD
  is essential to knowing how to interpret it.
- CFD Property #1 is that the top line of a Cumulative
  Flow Diagram *always* represents the cumulative
  arrivals to a process. The bottom line on a CFD
  always represents the cumulative departures from
  a process.
- CFD Property #2 is that due to its cumulative nature, no line on a CFD can ever decrease (go down).

- The best way to capture data for a CFD is to track the date at which an item enters each step of your process workflow. You are going to need those data points for other analysis anyway, so you might as well collect those from the start.
- Three easy ways to spot if a CFD has not been constructed properly:
    - If any line on the chart slopes downward on any part of the graph.
    - If something that sounds like a "backlog" has been graphed (remember, a visualized backlog may not necessarily be bad—but it usually is!).
    - If some type of projection has been plotted.

Chapter 5 - Flow Metrics and CFDs

The reason I was so pedantic about how to correctly collect data to build CFDs in the previous chapter is because only with a properly constructed CFD can we accurately perform the analysis techniques that we need for predictability. Those techniques are precisely what I plan to present in this chapter and the next. We begin our discussion with some quantitative analysis.

Work In Progress

Since the top line of a CFD represents the cumulative arrivals of items to our process, and the bottom line of a CFD represents the cumulative departures of items from our system, then the vertical difference between those two lines at any reporting interval represents the total Work In Progress in the system. As you have probably figured out, this principle can easily be extended such that we can measure the Work In Progress between any two points in the system at any point in time. That is to say, we can quickly measure the Work In Progress in the Analysis Active step, in the Development Done step, or the total Work In Progress between Analysis Done and Test (just to name a few examples). Thus, our next fundamental principle of CFDs is:

 CFD Property #3: The vertical distance between any two lines on a CFD is the total amount of work that is in progress between the two workflow steps represented by the two chosen lines.

Figure 5.1 shows the total WIP as 90 work items on September 1:

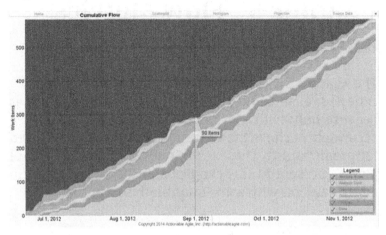

Figure 5.1: Reading Total Work In Progress off of a CFD

In this example, we got to the number 90 by subtracting the number of work items (or y-value) of the bottom line of the CFD on September 1 from the number of work items of the top line on September 1. Specifically, the bottom line on the chart shows a value of 200 work items on September 1. The top line shows a value of 290 work items on September 1. Subtracting the bottom line number of work items from the top line number of work items (290 – 200) gives us a total WIP of 90 work items.

Reading WIP off of each step in the workflow is accomplished in much the same way as shown in Figure 5.2:

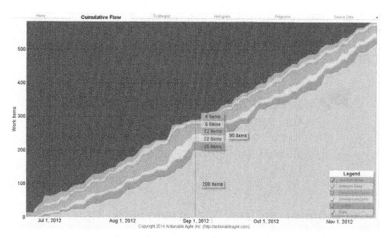

Figure 5.2: Reading WIP at Each Step of the Workflow

The calculation of these numbers was performed in exactly the same way as the total WIP calculation; i.e., by subtracting the y-value of the bottom line of a given band from the y-value of the top line of a given band.

Approximate Average Cycle Time

Continuing the same example, the horizontal difference between the top line of a CFD and bottom line of a CFD at any point along the graph is your process's *Approximate Average Cycle Time*. To approximately calculate how long—on average—it took for items to complete at a particular reporting interval, we choose the point on the bottom line of the CFD that corresponds with the date that we are interested in, and then we draw a horizontal line backward until it intersects the top line of the CFD. We then look to see what date corresponds with that top line intersection and subtract it from the date we just got from the bottom line. This subtraction will give you the Approximate Average Cycle Time for the items that finished on the bottom line date of interest.

This leads us to the next fundamental property of CFDs:

 CFD Property #4: The horizontal distance between any two lines on a CFD represents the Approximate Average Cycle Time for items that finished between the two workflow steps represented by the chosen two lines.

Continuing on from the previous example, let's say we want to know what the Approximate Average Cycle Time was for items that finished on September 1st. In this case our calculation would look like Figure 5.3:

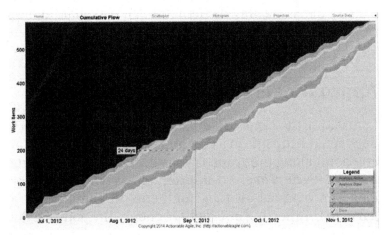

Figure 5.3: Overall Process Approximate Average Cycle Time Calculation

In this example, to calculate the Approximate Average Cycle Time for stories that finished on September 1 (which is this example is 24 days), you perform the following steps. (Please note that in this case the reporting interval is days. These steps would be the same for whatever time unit you choose to report your data; e.g., weeks, months, etc.):

1. Start with date you are interested in on the bottom line of the graph. In this case, that date is September 1.
2. Draw a horizontal line backward from that point on the bottom line until the line intersects a point on the top line of the CFD.
3. Read the date value of the top line of the CFD at that intersection point. In this case that date is August 9.
4. Subtract top line date from the bottom line date. In this case, September 1 minus August 9 is 23 days.
5. Add 1 to the result. In this case, 23 plus 1 is 24 days.

Why add one day in Step #5? I always advise the addition of one "time unit" (in this case that time unit is days) because I would argue the shortest amount of time that an item can take to complete is one unit. For example, if a given work item starts and completes on the same day (e.g., September 1), what is its Cycle Time? If we were just to subtract September 1 from September 1 we would get a Cycle Time of zero days. I think that result is misleading. After all, zero days suggests that no time whatsoever was spent completing that item. That is not reflective of reality which is why one day needs to be added. Further, the addition of one day makes the calculation more inclusive. For example, if a work item starts on September 1 and finishes on September 2, what is its Cycle Time? If all we did is subtract those two dates, we would get a Cycle Time of one day. But I would suggest that since time was spent on that item on both September 1 *and* September 2 that the more representative Cycle Time is two days. Which means that we would again need to add one day to our calculation. You might disagree with this advice for your own particular situation. And that is ok (as long as you are consistent in your calculations). You will just want to note, though, that all Cycle Time calculations in this book follow the "addition of one time unit" rule.

Getting back to our original discussion, the fact that you can draw a horizontal line on a CFD and subtract two dates to come up with an Approximate Average Cycle time should be amazing to you for a couple of reasons. The first is that to normally calculate an average you simply add up a whole bunch of values and then divide by the total number of values that you have added up. However, in this case all we are doing is subtracting two dates to come up with an average. Seems strange that that would work, but it does.

The second reason that this result is remarkable, is that the items that started in the Analysis Active column (the first column on the board) are not necessarily the stories that have finished in the Done column (the last column on the board), yet this calculation will still yield an Approximate Average Cycle Time. Interestingly enough, how good an approximation this calculation is will depend on how well we are adhering to the assumptions that make Little's Law work.

As with the Work In Progress calculation, this property can also be extended to handle the calculation between any two arbitrary points on your chart. That means we can draw horizontal lines to calculate the Approximate Average Cycle Time through Analysis Active, or through Test, or the Approximate Average Cycle Time from Analysis Done through Development Done (again, to name a few examples). Pictorially, some of these examples would look like Figure 5.5:

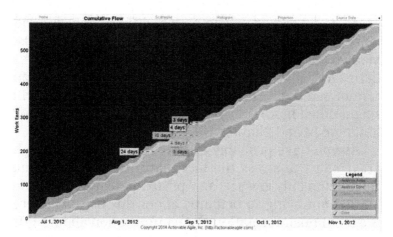

Figure 5.5: Approximate Average Cycle Times at Each Step in the Workflow

Note that this calculation is only valid for items that have finished. That is to say, this horizontal line that you draw to make this calculation must begin at the top line of the bottom band at the reporting interval that you are interested in and be drawn "backward" until it intersects the top line. Starting at the top line and drawing a line "forward" could cause you to never intersect the top line of the bottom-most band. The implication here is that CFDs are only good at exploring what already has happened in your process. This point is so important that I am going to call it out as its own property of CFDs:

 CFD Property #5: The data displayed on a CFD depicts only what *has* happened for a given process. Any chart that shows any type of projection is not a CFD.

Again, I am not saying here that projections are not important—far from it. All I am saying is that projections forward about what will or could happen in your process will require a completely different chart—and more probably a completely different approach (like Monte Carlo Simulation). Just know that we cannot use CFDs for that forecasting purpose or that, if you do, you cannot call the resulting projection graph a CFD. I will spend much more time on projections later in the book (Chapter 14 and Chapter 15).

As you have probably noticed, I have gone through great pains to stress the fact that this horizontal line calculation only gives us an Approximate Average Cycle Time. I am being so pedantic about this because there is a lot of misinformation or disinformation about CFDs out there. If you were to go out and do some research on Cumulative Flow Diagrams, you will probably find that many people will tell you that doing this horizontal line calculation will give you an exact Cycle Time. It does not. The reason is because the items that start on the top line of your Cumulative Flow Diagram (at the beginning of your horizontal line) are not necessarily the items that finish at the bottom line of your Cumulative Flow Diagram (at the end of your horizontal line). Therefore, it would be impossible to calculate an exact Cycle Time for those items using just the diagram alone. Further, some people will tell you that this horizontal line calculation will lead to an exact *average* Cycle Time. This statement is also potentially incorrect. Unless we go in and look at the data that was used to generate the chart, or we have an understanding of some of the policies that have been put in place to generate the diagram the best we can say is that this horizontal calculation will lead to an Approximate Average Cycle Time. However, this approximation can be very good. In Chapters 5-7, I will explain some policies that you can put in place within your own team, or your own process, such that this calculation will give you an excellent approximation.

There is another great (potentially most important) reason to understand why this horizontal line represents only an Approximate Average Cycle Time. It turns out the comparison of the Approximate Average Cycle Time off of your CFD with the exact average Cycle Time from your real data can give you tremendous insight as to the health of your process. We will get into the specifics of that calculation and analysis in Chapter 9.

Average Throughput

If the bottom line of your CFD represents the departures from your process, then the slope of that line between any two points (reporting intervals) is your *exact* average Throughput between those two points. This slope calculation is the very same "rise over run" calculation that you may remember from your previous mathematics training (it is ok if you do not remember as I have included an example of this calculation in the discussion after Figure 5.6). Furthermore, just to be clear, this is indeed an exact average Throughput calculation, not an approximate average as in the Cycle Time calculation above.

Likewise, if the slope of the bottom line of the CFD is your average Throughput, then the slope of the top-most line is your average arrival rate. The slope of that top line represents how fast work is coming into our system, while the slope of the bottom line represents how fast work leaving our system.

This leads to the last of our fundamental properties of Cumulative Flow Diagrams:

CFD Property #6: The slope of any line between any two reporting intervals on a CFD
represents the exact Average Arrival Rate
of the process state represented by the succeeding band.

As you have probably already guessed, Property #6 is a direct result of Property #1, but it is so important that I wanted to call it out on its own. One important corollary to this property is that the slope of any line also represents the exact average Throughput (or Departure Rate or Completion Rate) for the preceding workflow step.

To visualize this result, let's continue to look at the same example that we used in the WIP and Cycle Time sections (Figure 5.1). To calculate the Throughput of the overall process, we simply compute the slope of the bottom line of the CFD (the top line of the Done state in Figure 5.6). Likewise, to calculate the arrival rate we use the same slope calculation for Analysis Active line. Both situations are shown in Figure 5.6:

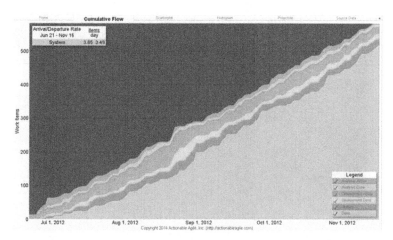

Figure 5.6: Arrival Rate and Departure Rate on a CFD

To calculate Average Throughput you will first need to ascertain the date range you are interested in. In this example (Figure 5.6) that date range is June 21 – November 16. The number of days in that range is our "run", or, in this case, November 16 minus June 21 equals 148 days. Second, we need to figure the "rise" of our bottom line work item data over that date range. The number of items on the bottom line at June 21 is zero and the number of items on the bottom line at Nov 16 is 517. Subtracting those two numbers gives us our "rise", or in this case 517 – 0 = 517. To calculate Average Throughput, then, you simply divide the rise by the run. In this case, our Average Throughput is 517 divided by 148 which equals 3.49 items per day. You can perform the exact same calculation for Average Arrival rate by substituting the data for the top line of the CFD into your rise over run formula.

Just as with WIP and Cycle Time, we can perform the slope calculations to get the Average Arrival or Average Departure rate for any step of the workflow as shown in Figure 5.7:

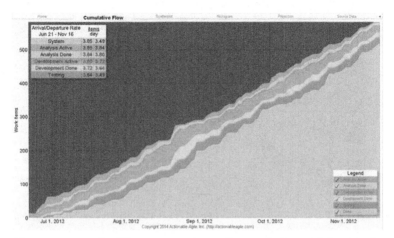

Figure 5.7: Arrival/Departure Rates for Each Step of the Work-flow

Conclusion

As you can see, one of the things that makes CFDs so powerful is that you can easily visualize and/or compute all the important metrics of flow mentioned in Chapter 2 off of just one diagram. Putting it all together pictorially is shown in Figure 5.8:

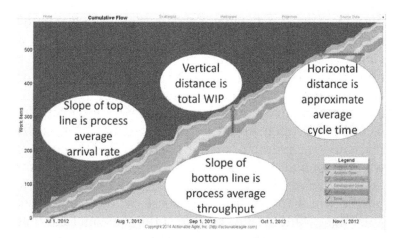

Figure 5.8: The Three Basic Metrics of Flow on a CFD

Numerically, these calculations look like Figure 5.9:

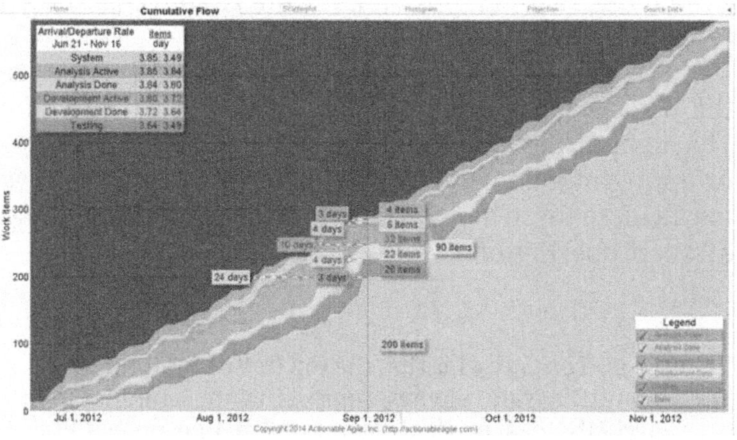

Figure 5.9: Numerical Representations of the Metrics of Flow

As I mentioned in Chapter 2, it is possible to segment WIP into several constituent types (as also mentioned in Chapter 3 on Little's Law). CFDs are no different. As you may have guessed by now, when we collect our flow data, we can either look at that dataset as a whole in a

CFD, or we can construct a CFD based on only one or more of the subtypes. For example, we can look at a single CFD that shows just the data for the user story type, or we can build a CFD based on just defects, or we can generate a CFD that combines both user stories and maintenance—to just name a few. This property of CFDs will open up all kinds of avenues of analysis for you. For example, at the portfolio level, you may want to look at data combined across all teams, or you may just want to filter based on an individual team. Or maybe you want to filter by release. At the team level, you might want to filter by some other custom field that is particularly relevant to your context (as in the "bad data" example from above). All of these activities are perfectly ok and I would challenge you to think about what data attributes you might want to collect and then filter on when analyzing your CFDs.

CFDs offer a concise way to simultaneously visualize the three basic metrics of flow: WIP, Cycle Time, and Throughput (albeit sometimes in the form of averages or approximate averages). You can only be guaranteed to calculate these metrics, however, if your graph obeys all six properties of a CFD:

CFD Property #1 is that the top line of a Cumulative Flow Diagram always represents the cumulative arrivals to a process. The bottom line on a CFD always represents the cumulative departures from a process.

CFD Property #2 is that due to its cumulative nature, no line on a CFD can ever decrease (go down).

CFD Property #3 is that the vertical distance between any two lines on a CFD is the total amount of work that is in progress between the two workflow steps represented by the two chosen lines.

CFD Property #4 is that the horizontal distance between any two lines on a CFD represents the Approximate Average Cycle Time for items that finished between the two workflow steps represented by the chosen two lines.

CFD Property #5 is that the data displayed on a CFD depicts only what has happened for a given process. Any chart that shows any type of projection is not a CFD.

CFD Property #6 is that the slope of any line between any two reporting intervals on a CFD represents the exact Average Arrival Rate of the process state represented by the succeeding band.

With a strong quantitative understanding of CFDs, we move now to a more qualitative analysis—which is really where the predictability rubber hits the road.

Key Learnings and Takeaways

- CFD Property #3: The vertical distance between any two lines on a CFD is the total amount of work that is in progress between the two workflow steps represented by the two chosen lines.
- CFD Property #4: The horizontal distance between any two lines on a CFD represents the Approximate Average Cycle Time for items that finished between the two workflow steps represented by the chosen two lines.
- CFD Property #5: The data displayed on a CFD depicts only what *has* happened for a given process.

Any chart that shows any type of projection is not a CFD.

- CFD Property #6: The slope of any line between any two reporting intervals on a CFD represents the exact Average Arrival Rate of the process state represented by the succeeding band.
- A CFD is only a CFD if it obeys all six properties because only by following all of these properties can you be guaranteed to derive the correct quantitative metrics of flow off of your graph.
- Consider building CFDs that show both "Active" and "Done" states within workflow steps. For example, if your "Development" workflow step if further segmented into "Active" and "Done", then think about showing both of those sub columns on your CFD.
- Some common myths about CFDs:
  - It is always correct to build a CFD from work item count data at each reporting interval.
  - A horizontal line represents an exact Cycle Time or an exact average Cycle Time.
  - It is always ok to represent a traditional backlog on a CFD.
  - It is possible to make a qualitative assessment of a CFD without understanding its context.

Chapter 6 - Interpreting CFDs

Now that you have a good grasp of how to do basic quantitative analysis on a CFD, you will see that you have already built an intuition around how to spot qualitative flow problems without doing any computations. An exploration of how to interpret a Cumulative Flow Diagram is what this chapter is all about.

First, though, some words of warning. The most important thing to remember about any qualitative analysis of CFDs is that the diagrams themselves are very context specific. If you look at a CFD without understanding the context in which it was created, then all you are doing is looking at a picture. Just like any visualization, a CFD is not going to tell you exactly what is wrong with your process or exactly how to fix it, but it is going to shine a light or a magnifying glass on the places to investigate.

To that point, you will be tempted to jump to snap judgments the next time you see a Cumulative Flow Diagram. Do not. This is the trap that most knowledge work blog posts and other publications on CFDs fall into. Be better than that! The reason we visualize flow on a CFD is not so that we can draw superficial conclusions about what is wrong with a given process. Rather, the reason we visualize flow via a CFD is so that we can begin to ask the right questions sooner. CFDs are not going to do our jobs for us. They do not replace thinking.

One last thing: it may seem strange, but doing any qualitative analysis on CFDs really requires sound knowledge of how to do quantitative analysis on CFDs. If you have skipped ahead to this chapter because you assumed you knew CFDs, you may want to go back and read both Chapter 4 and Chapter 5.

Keeping all that in mind, let's take a look at some common CFDs patterns and explore what questions we might ask when we see these shapes emerge.

Mismatched Arrivals and Departures

Let's say we had a CFD that looked like:

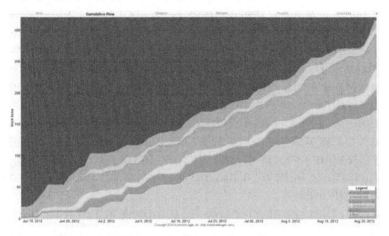

Figure 6.1: Mismatched Arrivals and Departures

In this picture the slope of the top-most line is steeper than the slope of the bottom-most line. This is a classic pattern that develops whenever items arrive to our process faster than they depart. Most companies that I visit that struggle with predictability have a CFD that looks something like this.

Why is this so bad? Any time that we have items that arrive to our process faster than items depart from our process means that WIP will grow over time. In Chapter

3 on Little's Law, we learned that an increase in WIP will almost certainly lead to an increase in Cycle Time (recall from that chapter that having arrival rate equal departure rate—on average—is one of the key assumptions for Little's Law to work). It is impossible to be predictable in a world where WIP constantly increases and Cycle Times elongate.

By definition, a process that exhibits a shape similar to Figure 6.1 is unstable. Process stability is fundamental to process predictability. So much so that I will devote all of the next chapter (Chapter 7) to explaining some causes and some remedies whenever the arrivals to your process exceed departures.

Flat Lines

Another pattern that I look for on a CFD is whenever any lines that flatten out over long periods of time (remember that lines can never go down!). Figure 6.2 shows an example of this:

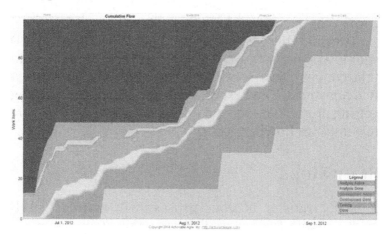

Figure 6.2: Flat Throughput Sections on a CFD

Depending on your perspective, these lines could represent either periods of zero arrivals or periods of zero departures. Usually you will be concerned about these flat lines as periods of zero departures. The reason why is because zero departures means nothing is getting done. In other words, no value is being delivered to the customer (or to a downstream step).

There are all kinds of circumstances that could cause this pattern to emerge. Maybe there is a period of several public holidays where most of the staff is out (the two weeks around Christmas and New Year's in the U.S. is a good example). Maybe the team is blocked by some external event such as the whole test environment being down such that testing cannot complete.

Whatever the reason, think about what this zero Throughput is doing to your predictability. If a horizontal line represents an Approximate Average Cycle Time on your CFD, what do you think is happening to that approximation during periods of long, flat Throughput? What happens when we plug in a zero for average Throughput in Little's Law, but average WIP is non-zero? What does that do to Cycle Time?

The point here is that an emergent flat line on a CFD should trigger some type of urgent conversation and that conversation should be about answering at least two questions. The first question is "Why isn't anything getting done?" The second question is "What can we do to get things flowing again?"

Stair Steps

A batch transfer in your process will manifest itself as "stair steps" on your CFD. By stair steps I mean a flat period on a line (as discussed above) immediately followed by a jump up in arrival rate as illustrated in Figure 6.3:

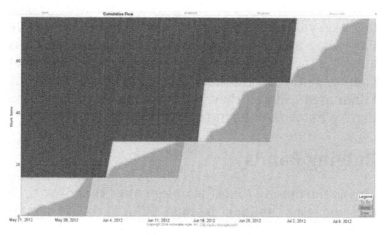

Figure 6.3: Batch on a CFD

For example, if your team has a reporting interval of every day on your CFD, but—for whatever reason—you wait five days to replenish the input column on your board. What you will see on your chart is five straight days of a flat input line followed by an immediate increase when the column is replenished. Similarly, what if the bottom line of your CFD represents a deployment to production, but you only do that deployment every three months? What is that going to look like on your CFD?

Some references you may have read suggest that these stair steps are caused by a regular cadence—but they do not have to be. Any batch transfer—whether due to a regular cadence or not—will cause these stair steps to form. If due to a regular cadence, then the stair steps will be of roughly uniform size and shape. Non-regular batch transfer will usually have a more uneven appearance to the steps. Both of those situations are shown in Figure 6.3.

It is important to note here, that batch in and of itself is not necessarily a bad thing. What you will need to do when you see stair steps appear on your Cumulative Flow Diagram is to have a think about how batch is affecting (positively or negatively) the predictability of your system. Can those periods of batch be reduced? Eliminated? Should they be? What would it take to do that? What would the impact to Cycle Time be?

Bulging Bands

This is the one that most teams go after first. Any time that you see a "bulging" band in a CFD, it clearly signals an explosion of WIP in that particular workflow step. An example of this is shown in Figure 6.4:

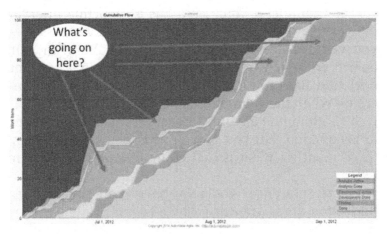

Figure 6.4: Bulging Bands on a CFD

We know that large WIP is bad because it almost always results in longer Cycle Times and poorer pre-dictability. The obvious question we need to ask is, "what is causing our increased WIP"? As always, that answer will depend on your specific situation. Maybe the team is simply ignoring WIP limits and starting new work arbitrarily. Maybe several key team members have gone on holiday for extended periods of time. Maybe work is progressing slowly due to poor requirements or poor design. Any of these and more might explain any of the bulging bands in Figure 6.4. What are some of the causes for a pile up of work at your job?

One thing to look out for in these situations, though, is that the cause of the increased WIP may not necessarily be found in the workflow step where the bulge appears. It could be due to a "push" from a previous step, or it could be cause by some blockage in one or more downstream steps. Do not be lulled into thinking the problem is always in the obvious place.

Additionally, remember earlier when I suggested that you should consider separating your workflow steps into "Active" and "Done" and then you should graph each of those sub-steps on your CFD? One reason I recommend that approach is because those "Done" sub-steps are clearly queuing columns—i.e., they are columns where no value add work is happening; work is just sitting there waiting to be pulled. I mention this now because while a bulging band in general is bad, a bulging band in a queuing step can be especially bad. Ideally, the bands on the CFDs that represent the queuing states should be as thin as possible (I just told you why). Whenever those bands are constantly thick or whenever they bulge, then that pattern is suggesting something is going wrong with our process.

Disappearing Bands

Bands that disappear altogether on a Cumulative Flow Diagram could be telling us one of several things. The first possibility is that the reporting interval that we have chosen is too big. Consider, for example, that we choose a reporting period of every week for our chart. Let's further say that the work in our Test column flows through very quickly (e.g., in a day or two). In this case it is very likely that on any given reporting interval there will be zero Work In Progress in the test column such that the test band on the CFD will not show up. An example of bands disappearing is depicted in Figure 6.5:

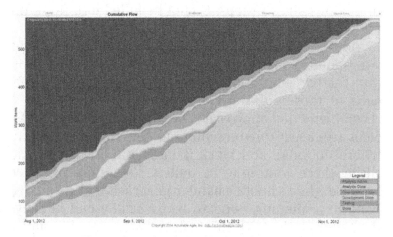

Figure 6.5: Disappearing Bands on a CFD

A second cause for a disappearing band may be that some upstream variability in our process is causing downstream steps to be starved.

Another possibility, is that the team frequently decides to skip a certain step in the workflow altogether resulting in that step not having any Work In Progress at any given time. For example, it could be near the end of a release and the team has decided to skip the Test step in the workflow, deciding instead to push work directly from Development into production. It would be up to you to decide given your particular context whether this is good or bad. While obviously an exaggerated case, in this instance the Test band on the CFD would completely disappear—much like what is shown in Figure 6.5.

The S-Curve

Remember in the last chapter when I talked about the special case of Little's Law when system WIP is allowed to go to zero? I gave two classic examples of when this might happen. First, a project usually begins with zero WIP and (ideally) ends with zero WIP. At a more granular level, an ideal Scrum sprint starts with zero WIP and ends with zero WIP.

I mention these examples again as the typical pattern that emerges on CFD between any two time instances of zero WIP is something called an "S-curve". An S-curve is characterized by a flat beginning section, followed by a steep middle section, and finishing again with a flat end period. This flat, then steep, then flat pattern is what gives the graph its distinctive "S" shape as in Figure 6.6:

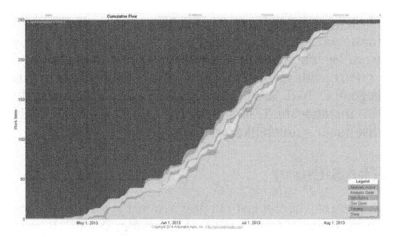

Figure 6.6: An S-Curve on a CFD

The phenomena that causes this "S" pattern to emerge is beyond the scope of this section, but know that, as I have just stated, it usually happens between any two time instances when WIP is allowed to go to zero. The reason I mention this now is think about what this S-curve does from a predictability standpoint. In this context, do you think it is always easy to match arrival and departure rates? Is it even possible?

Take it a step further. From a predictability perspective, do you think that it is optimal to manage projects this way (remember, I am talking about predictability here, not necessarily about how accounting or finance sees the world)? Do you think it is predicatively optimal to multiply this effect several times during the course of a project by breaking it up into several zero WIP-bounded sprints? How might we become more predictable day to day, week to week, month to month by never allowing WIP to go to zero?

For example, in Figure 6.6 how do you think the team is doing at matching arrivals to departures at both the beginning and end of this time period? Whether reasonable or not, what we can say is that those flat spots add inefficiencies and kill predictability. Is there a better way to manage work such that we do not have those start-stops and flat lines?

Just something to think about...

A Boring CFD

Suppose you have a CFD like Figure 6.7:

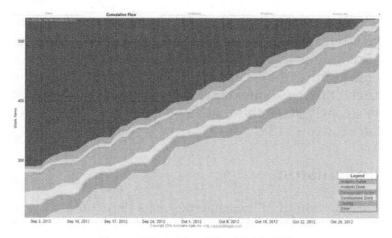

Figure 6.7: A "Good-Looking" CFD

Everything looks rather good, right? If it truly is, then it is time to start asking questions about other process improvement actions we might take. For example, is it possible to get the lines even closer together by reducing WIP and thus improving Cycle Time? What can we do to make the Throughput line steeper?

The thing is, it is possible to get a very pretty CFD picture but still have a very dysfunctional process underneath. The best example of this is the accumulation of Flow Debt. But that topic is so important that it deserves its own chapter as well (see Chapter 9).

You may have noticed that I have not explicitly mentioned anything about using CFDs to spot bottlenecks in your process. That omission was on purpose. It is because I am dubious about that approach. This may surprise you as if you have read anything about CFDs, you have probably read how useful they are to spot bottlenecks. I do not agree with this language. I believe that the best you can do by just looking at a CFD is to pose some questions about some variability that may be occurring. It is impossible to spot a systemic bottleneck. This may seem like a subtle distinction to you, but I prefer Deming's and Shewhart's language of variability to that of Goldratt's language of the Theory of Constraints. I think you will get much more bang for the buck thinking about knowledge work in this way. I feel so strongly about this that I a chapter to this discussion later (Chapter 13).

Conclusion

A discussion of all possible patterns that could emerge on a CFD would be a whole book in itself (hmmm...good idea). What I have given you here are some of the more common things you will come across. I am hoping you will use these examples along with your quantitative analysis knowledge to discover the right questions to ask sooner. Remember that the point of CFD analysis is not just about looking at a pretty picture. The point is to look at the graph in the context in which it was generated and have a discussion about what the patterns mean to overall process performance and predictability. Thus, the real purpose for analyzing a CFD is to learn. You learn by asking questions. "What's going on with our flow?" "Is it a good thing or bad thing?" "If good, how can we keep doing it?" "If bad, what interventions can we take to make things better?" A CFD not only gets you asking the right questions sooner, but will also suggest the right actions to take for increased predictability.

I started my discussion of CFDs by saying that not only is most of the information out there in the Agile-o-sphere incorrect concerning these charts, but also that all tools that I have come across (at the time of this writing) generate these graphs incorrectly (save the one which I will discuss in a minute). So what are you to do?

One option is to capture the data manually as I have outlined here and generate the chart yourself using something like Excel. This is a reasonable approach and one that many teams utilize. The problem with Excel is it is not a very dynamic or interactive way to analyze the data. It also becomes cumbersome as your dataset gets very large.

The second option is to use the ActionableAgile™ Analytics tool. This tool was built for the sole purpose of the advanced analysis of these metrics of flow. At the risk of putting forth a shameless plug, the ActionableAgile™ Analytics tool was created by my company, so you can be sure that any and all charts that are created by it are generated correctly (the ActionableAgile™ Analytics tool is also great tool for generating Cycle Time Scatterplots—I will discuss Scatterplots in Chapters 10-12).

There is a lot of chatter out there about the uselessness of Cumulative Flow Diagrams. Those discussions are disappointing because a lot of these comments come from well-known persons within the industry. Obviously, I am biased so all I want to suggest is that after reading this chapter (and this book) you will make your own mind up about the utility of CFDs. I am hoping to have persuaded you otherwise by the time you finish.

The last thing to note is that the predictive power of

your CFDs depends almost entirely on how well your process obeys the assumptions behind Little's Law (Chapter 3). This point is so important, that the next three chapters will explain how to spot violations of Little's Law on your charts and what you can do to correct them.

Key Learnings and Takeaways

- On your CFD, does arrival rate match departure rate?
- Are there any bulges in the workflow step bands?
- Do any bands disappear?
- Are there any long periods of flat lines?
- Are there stair steps?
- Is there an S-curve?
- Think about improvements to consider if everything looks good on your CFD.

Chapter 7 - Conservation of Flow Part I

Imagine, for a second, an airport where the rate at which planes landed far exceeded the rate at which planes took off. Very little further imagination is needed to come to the conclusion that, in this scenario, the total number of planes situated at the airport would dramatically increase over time. It would not be too long before all the available gates at the airport became occupied and that air traffic control (ATC) would be forced to find creative places to park the extra aircraft. If the situation continued, sooner or later all reasonable space at the airport would fill up, including utilizing any space available on active runways. As soon as runways were occupied, no new planes would be able to land nor would any planes scheduled for departure be able to take off.

Obviously, in the real world, air traffic control does everything it can to avoid this nightmare scenario. It is for this precise reason why if a certain airport—let's say Chicago's O'Hare (ORD)—is experiencing weather or some other reduction of capacity, that ATC slows down planes in the air headed to ORD or they put a ground stop on all other airports that have aircraft scheduled to travel to ORD. Anyone who travels with any amount of regularity has probably experienced an incident like this. You can bet that ATC is closely monitoring and managing the rate at which planes take off at any given airport and they are doing everything they can to match that take off rate to the pace at which planes land.

You do not have to think too long to come up with

many similar examples. The principle remains the same: any time you try to shove items into a system at a faster rate than items can exit the system, you are met with disastrous consequences. This principle seems immediately obvious and intuitive. Yet, for whatever reason, we constantly ignore this rule when we manage knowledge work. It is exactly this phenomenon that Little's Law assumption #1 is trying to address. Remember from Chapter 3 that:

 Little's Law Assumption #1: The average input or Arrival Rate of a process should equal the average output or Departure Rate.

Stated in more layman's terms, Little's Law demands that we only start work at about the same rate at which we finish old work (on average). Assumption #1 constitutes the first part of a principle known of the Conservation of Flow (CoF). Any time that flow is not conserved, predictability suffers.

Defining Arrivals

To understand if flow is not being conserved in your process, you first need to clearly define an arrival point, and clearly define departure point. I refer you once again to Figure 2.1 (the queuing system diagram from Chapter 2). To apply CoF to predictability, we must design a system that clearly mimics what is going on in that diagram.

Let's consider arrivals first. That is, we need to establish an explicit and obvious entry point where teams can pull in new work such that it is counted as WIP. This entry point usually takes the form of a WIP-limited column on the front of your process, and you will normally see this column labeled as "Input" or "Ready" or "To Do" or the like (more on how to set the WIP limit on this column a little later in this chapter). An example of what this column might look like is shown in Figure 7.1:

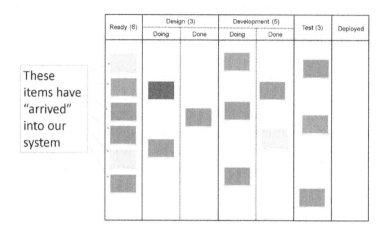

Figure 7.1: Arrivals into a Kanban System

In Figure 7.1, items that have been placed onto the "Ready" column are said to have arrived into the process. This column represents a clear, unambiguous signal to the world that the team has accepted work.

Please note that this arrivals column is very different from a more traditional backlog. It is not meant to be an ever-expanding repository for all candidate customer requests. The WIP Limit on this column represents the real-time capacity of the system to take on new work, and serves to force us to only pull in new work in a just-in-time manner. This is one of the reasons why—as I stated in Chapter 5—that this Ready column would be displayed on a CFD while the backlog would not.

We implicitly stated a couple of policies here, so let's make those policies explicit. First, we have said that work items are only considered to have arrived into

our system once they are placed onto our "arrivals"
column (the "Ready" column in Figure 7.1). Second, this
arrivals column will have a WIP limit on it and that
we will only pull new work into the system when that
WIP limit signals that we have capacity to do so. And
third, since work can only arrive via this first column,
the downstream steps of our process can only consider
pulling work from there.

Since what we are ultimately looking for is an understanding of the rate of arrivals into the system, then
measuring that rate now simply becomes a matter of
counting the number of new work items placed onto
that arrivals column per unit time. The unit or interval
of time you choose is completely up to you (day, week,
every two weeks), but one thing you must keep in mind
is that the unit of time you choose to measure the Arrival
Rate must match the unit of time that you choose to measure your Departure Rate (I will discuss Departure Rate
shortly). Thus, if you measure Arrival Rate in weeks,
then you should also measure the Departure Rate in
weeks.

A very subtle but very important point to note here
is that choosing the same interval of time to measure
arrivals and departures does not mean that the cadence
of arrivals and departures must be the same. For example, your team could choose to deploy to production
at a cadence of every two weeks, but could also choose
to replenish the input column every week. Not only
is staggering cadences like that perfectly acceptable, it
might be optimal given your specific context. However,
it makes comparing Arrival Rates and Departure Rates
slightly more complicated. If your Throughput data is in
terms of two week intervals and your arrival data is in
terms of one week intervals, then you will have to do
some conversion to get them to the same unit of time.

Whether you choose to convert Throughput data from two week periods to one week periods or whether you choose to convert arrival data from one week to two week periods is completely up to you. Just know that whatever unit of time you choose for your reporting must be consistent across all metrics. It will be an interesting and important exercise for you to figure out the optimal reporting interval for your specific context.

Defining Departures

In a similar fashion, we are going to need to establish a clear, unambiguous departure point for our system. Items that pass this point do not necessarily have to be visualized—though most teams do choose to dedicate space on their board for departures—but they do need to be counted. If the departure column is visualized, then you will normally see it with the title "Done" or "Deployed" or the like. Typically speaking, if a team chooses to represent the departures column on their board, then it will not have a WIP Limit on it. Regardless of the visualization employed, it is important to define the exact point of the system where work departs, (hopefully) never to return. For example, this could be the point where we deploy code to production or the point at which we hand an item off to a downstream team (see Figure 7.2).

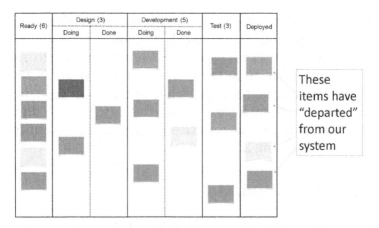

Figure 7.2: Items that have departed from the system

In Figure 7.2, the demarcation line between "in our process" and "not in our process" is the line that separates the "Test" column from the "Deployed" column. More importantly, the expectation here is that the team has put in place a set of policies for what it means for items to move from Test to Deployed, and that once those items are in Deployed, they no longer count against the capacity of the team; i.e., they no longer count as WIP.

Measuring the rate of departures from the system is exactly the same as measuring the rate of arrivals. We simply count the number of work items placed into Deployed (that have "crossed the line" so to speak) per unit of time. Again, the unit or interval of time is not important, only that you match your departures interval to your arrivals interval as discussed above.

Once you have tracked your Arrival and Departure Rates for an arbitrarily long period of time (though the amount of time needed for "good" data might be much shorter than you think—perhaps as little as a few weeks), then you can average those two rates and compare them. If those two averages come out to be the same, then you are in good shape. My guess, though, is that your two average rates will be different. I am going to discuss what that difference means and some actions to take to correct them in a minute, but first I would like to talk about a better method for performing the above analysis.

Arrivals and Departures on a CFD

There is a much better way to visualize whether the Average Arrival Rate equals the Average Departure Rate for your system. This better method is to perform the preceding analysis using a Cumulative Flow Diagram.

Let's suppose we are running a Kanban board that looks like the one in Figure 7.3:

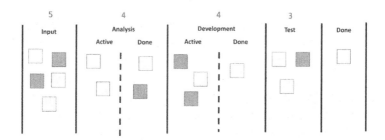

Figure 7.3: Example Kanban Board

Note that this particular team has chosen to name their arrivals column "Input", and that they have limited that column to five work items in progress at a time. Note also that the team has chosen to display the departures column and that they have labelled that column "Done". This departures column is WIP unlimited and the implication is that they have put in place explicit policies for what it means for items to be moved from "Test" to "Done".

So what might a CFD look like for a board like this? It might look like the one shown in Figure 7.4:

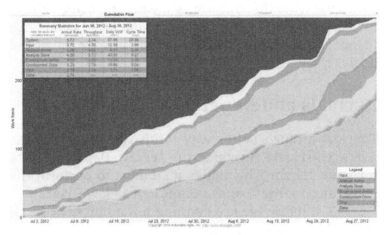

Figure 7.4: An Example CFD

From Chapter 4, we know that each layer of this CFD represents a step in the workflow of the Kanban board shown in Figure 7.3. We also know that the slope of the top line of the topmost layer represents the Arrival Rate of the process and the slope of the top line of the bottommost band represents the Departure Rate (or Throughput). You can see from Figure 7.4 that those rates have been calculated to be 3.72 items per day and 2.74 items per day for the Arrival and Departure Rates, respectively. This calculation tells us that items are arriving to the process faster than items are leaving the process at about the rate of one item per day. What might the implications of this situation be?

The nice thing about CFDs, however, is that we need not necessarily perform this quantitative analysis to see that something is going wrong with our system. CFDs are such a powerful visualization technique that we can quite quickly do a qualitative assessment of the health of our system.

For example, imagine you had CFD that looked like the one in Figure 7.5:

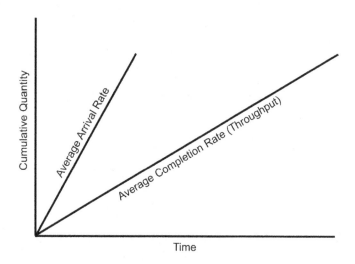

Figure 7.5: Quick Qualitative Assessment of CFD

It would not take you long to figure out that there was something wrong with your process. In this picture it is quite obvious—without doing any quantitative analysis—that work is arriving into your system at a much faster rate than work is departing from you system. A few paragraphs ago I asked you to think about the implication of this particular situation. To answer that question we need to reexamine how WIP and Cycle Time are visualized on CFDs. From Chapter 5, we know that WIP is the vertical distance between arrivals and departures and that Approximate Average Cycle Time is the horizontal distance between arrivals and departures. These properties are summed up in Figure 7.6:

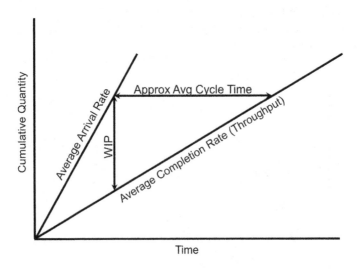

Figure 7.6: Flow Metrics on a CFD

But look what was going on earlier on in this diagram. When the Arrival Rate and Departure Rate lines were much closer together, you can see that WIP was much smaller and Approximate Average Cycle Times were much shorter. As arrivals continued to outpace departures—as the arrival line diverged from the departure line—the amount of WIP in the system got larger and larger and the Approximate Average Cycle Times got longer and longer (as shown in Figure 7.7).

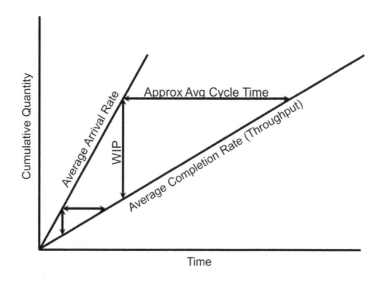

Figure 7.7: The Implication of Arrivals faster than Departures

In a situation like this, you have almost no chance at predictability. The actionable intervention suggested by a CFD that looks like Figure 5.5 is that we must get arrivals to match departures.

So how exactly do we get arrivals to match departures? The first thing we would do is to calculate the average Throughput off of the diagram. Let's say, for argument's sake, that we deploy items off our process at a cadence of once per week. Let's additionally say that the average Departure Rate of those deployed items comes out to five items per week (note here that we are choosing "week" as our unit of time). That number, five, gives us a clue as to what the WIP limit should be on our arrivals column. Since we are finishing five old items per week, that means we only want to start five new items per week. The implication here being that we would want to set a WIP Limit of five on the arrivals column (depending on the variability of our system, we might want to make that WIP Limit a little larger—say six or so—to make sure that our system is never starved for work). An important subtlety here is that the WIP Limit of five on the arrivals column assumes that you are replenishing the arrivals column at the same cadence as which you are deploying; i.e., once per week. But remember from before, that this need not be the case. If you wanted to replenish the input column once a day, then you would need to divide the original Arrival Rate number, five, by the number of times per week that you would do the replenishment (in this case five). Since five divided by five is one, then your new WIP limit on the arrivals column would be one.

Properly setting the WIP limit on the arrivals column will allow you to match the average Arrival Rate of items into your system with the average Departure Rate of items out of your system. When we do this, we will get a CFD that looks something like Figure 7.8:

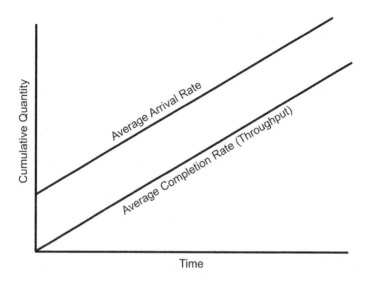

Figure 7.8: Average Arrival Rate equals Average Departure Rate

It should be immediately obvious from looking at the CFD in Figure 7.8 that the situation here is much better than that illustrated in Figure 7.5. As we will see in a subsequent chapter, having a pretty CFD is not a guarantee of a healthy system, but it is certainly a pretty decent start.

By the way, any time you expressly limit WIP throughout your workflow, and, more importantly, any time you honor the WIP limit(s) you have set, you will get a picture that looks like Figure 7.8. What I am saying is that you must operate a constant WIP style of pull system. Setting a WIP limit on the arrivals column is a necessary—but not sufficient—means to balancing arrivals and departures. For example, imagine that we have no explicit limit on our Test column but that we do have a WIP limit on the arrivals column. As work gets pulled (pushed, really) into Test because of the lack of a WIP limit, then that action will ultimately cause a pull of work from the arrivals column. Work getting pulled from the arrivals column will signal to the world that there is capacity to start new work and thus the arrivals column will be replenished even though no work has been completed. I hope it is easy to see that in this scenario how we can have items that arrive to our system faster than items that depart our system. So do not think your work is done by just limiting WIP at the front of your process. You must make sure that a constant amount of WIP (on average) is maintained throughout the whole process. Remember, the further you stray away from this principle, the less predictable you will be.

Limiting WIP on the arrivals column in the manner described here is one way to ensure that not too much work is started and just queuing at the beginning of your process. I have said it before, and I will say it again: delay is the enemy of flow. This approach will ensure a proper balance between having enough work to start such that your process is not starved and not having too much work such that work begins but just sits.

By the way, once we get a picture that looks like Figure 7.8, we will have taken the first—and probably most important—step to balance the demand on your system against the supply that your team can offer. We are now very far down the path to true process predictability.

Most Kanban boards have an explicit arrivals column at the front of the process, but this is by no means a requirement. It is completely reasonable that your particular work context allows your team to pull new work items in an immediate, ad hoc manner. That is to say, you need no coordination with any external stakeholder to prioritize items or you have a proxy for those stakeholders embedded with your team. In this case the arrivals column (e.g., the "To Do" or "Input" or "Ready" column) may be superfluous. This situation is perfectly ok. As I just mentioned, the way to match arrivals to departures in this context would be to make sure that a constant amount of WIP is maintained through the process at all times. Constant WIP could be maintained either by expressly limiting Work In Progress at each step of your work flow or by setting one global limit for the whole process (or some mixture of both). The point I am making here is that it does not really matter how you limit WIP throughout the whole system just as long as you do.

It should be said, though, that even in this particular situation a team could benefit from an arrivals column for many of reasons. Just know that an explicit arrivals column is neither prescribed nor required for predictable process design.

Conclusion

When you have a picture that looks like Figure 7.5 then your process is, by definition, unpredictable. The direct consequence of an Arrival Rate that exceeds a Departure Rate is a steady—if not dramatic—increase in WIP. Little's Law tells us that an increase in WIP will be matched by an increase in Cycle Time. The implication here is that if WIP grows unbounded, then Cycle Time will also essentially grow unbounded. If your Cycle Time is ever-increasing, then it becomes impossible to answer the question, "how long before this work item will done?"

In this chapter, I have purposefully not made any mention of how teams choose what particular items go on to the arrivals column at replenishment time. Nor have I made any mention of the order in which items should be pulled through the system once they have been placed on that column. These are very important questions and deserve ample consideration. The reason I have left those questions unanswered—for now—is that this chapter is simply about the mechanics of the first necessary step you need to take in order to stabilize your system and thus have any hope of predictability. Little's Law assumption #1 states that the average Arrival Rate to a system must equal the average Departure Rate of the system. I have shown you how to do that here. The answers to the replenishment and pull order questions will be addressed in the coming chapters.

I would argue that the arrivals column is one of—if not the most—important columns for your process design. In this chapter we have explored two very important reasons why this might be so:

1. The arrivals column acts as the throttle by which we constrain the amount of work that can arrive to our system at any given time. It is the mechanism by which we match the rate of arrivals in our process to the rate of departures. The matching of these rates is what is going to yield process predictability. And,

2. The arrivals column acts as our "commitment" point to start new work. The implication being that when new work is committed to, we expect it will flow completely through the process and depart the system. It is only when work departs our system that customer value can truly be recognized and our predictability be assessed.

In the real world, work item Cycle Times are not allowed to grow ad infinitum. Projects get cancelled and features get abandoned when they take too long to complete. This compounds the problem from a predictability perspective because not only is your Cycle Time not predictable, but now you cannot even be certain if a certain item that is started will ever finish. Items that start but never finish is yet another a violation of an assumption of Little's Law (do you remember which one?) that carries its own impacts on predictability. An exploration of that violation is where we will go next.

Key Learnings and Takeaways

- Little's Law assumption #1 says that the average input or Arrival Rate of a process should equal the average output or Departure Rate.
- Any predictable process needs a clear, unambiguous point at which it considers items to have "arrived".
- Any predictable process needs a clear, unambiguous point at which it considers items to have "departed".
- One of the best ways to visualize whether arrivals and departures are balanced is to visualize them via a CFD.
- To balance arrivals and departures is going to require limiting WIP not only at the arrivals column but also through the whole process.
- Once arrivals and departures are balanced, you have taken the necessary first (emphasis on first) step toward process predictability.
- Pretty CFD pictures could still mask underlying process problems.

Chapter 8 - Conservation of Flow Part II

I have never been skydiving, but I get the general gist. First, you pack a bunch of nylon into a little bag and strap that bag to your back. Then, you hop onto an airplane and fly up to a specified altitude. Finally, assuming you are insane, you jump out.

Other than the immediate commencement of a real-time experiment of Newton's Second Law of Motion, a very important thing happened to you once you jumped out of that airplane. Once outside the plane, you made a very real commitment to fall back down to the ground. Up until the moment of stepping off the plane, you had every opportunity to not make that commitment. You could have checked your parachute and found it was not packed properly. The plane could have not taken off due to bad weather. You could have decided not to jump because you were too scared. Any number of factors could have contributed to you not making that commitment.

Also notice that this commitment happened at the last responsible (possible) moment. Your jumping out of that airplane was a clear and unambiguous signal that you intended to fall back to earth.

Which brings us to my last point. Once outside the plane, you had every expectation that you were going to make it all the way down to the ground. The instant that you jumped it would take nothing short of an act of God to not get you back down to earth.

Whether you knew it or not, what you had just experienced in this situation was a perfect example of the second part of the Conservation of Flow (CoF). In the previous chapter, we discussed the first part of CoF, which also happened to be one of the necessary assumptions for Little's Law to work. In this chapter we will discuss the second part of CoF, which, as it so happens, is also one of the foundational assumptions of Little's Law:

 Little's Law Assumption #2: All work that is started will eventually be completed and exit (depart) the system.

The great benefit of implementing a pull system is that it is very easy to define what it means for work to have "started". A subtle side benefit that I have not talked much about until now is that pull systems also allow for us to perform just-in-time prioritizations and just-in-time commitments. It turns out that just-in-time prioritizations and just-in-time commitments are going to help us conserve flow.

Just-in-time Prioritization

I cannot tell you how many teams I have watched waste so much time, grooming, pruning, and re-prioritizing their backlogs. The truth is that the effort spent to maintain a backlog is waste. It is waste because the truth is that much of what goes into a backlog will never get worked on anyway. Why spend time prioritizing items that you have no clue nor confidence if or when they will ever get worked? Worse, when you are ready to start new work, new requirements will have shown up, or you will have gained new information, or both, which will require a whole reprioritization effort and will have rendered the previous prioritization activities moot.

Enter the concept of just-in-time prioritization. In a pull system, a prioritization conversation only happens when there is a clear indication that the team has capacity to do new work.

For example, let's look at a Kanban board (Figure 8.1) not unlike the one we discussed in the previous chapter:

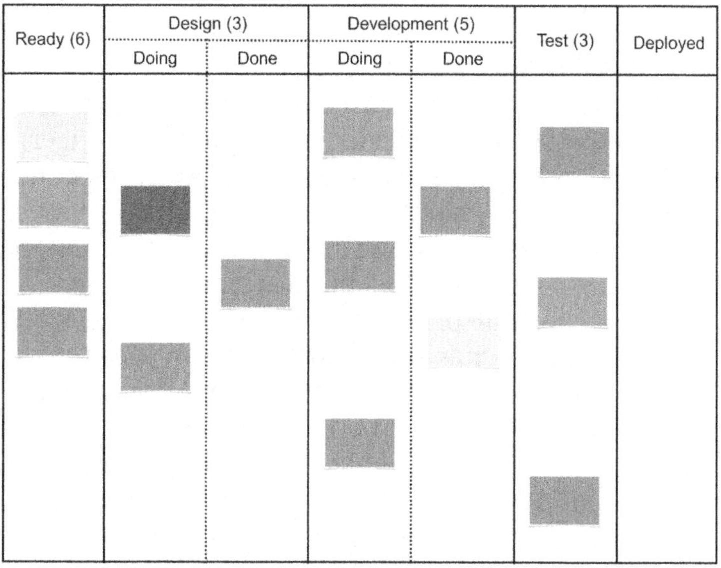

Ready (6)	Design (3)		Development (5)		Test (3)	Deployed
	Doing	Done	Doing	Done		

Figure 8.1: Just-in-time Prioritization

Notice that in Figure 8.1 the "Ready" or arrivals column has a Work In Progress limit of six. That means that the capacity of this process is such that a maximum of six new items can be started at any given time. What should this team do when they try to decide how many items to work on next? As they look at the board, they will see that there are already four items in the Ready column. Since the column already has four items in it, and since the WIP limit on the column is six, this means that the process is unambiguously signaling that the team only has capacity to start work on two new items. The prioritization conversation (i.e., which items should they choose) should then be focused only on "what are the next two most important items that we should start at this time?" Any discussion beyond deciding on just those two items is waste (e.g., having a conversation, say, about prioritizing the top ten items). Why? Because by the next time the team meets to replenish the Ready column, there will have been several things about the business environment that could have changed: business needs, customer feedback, regulatory concerns, etc. These changing factors will constantly feed new requirements the team's way and these continuously changing business needs means that the best strategy for prioritizing new work is in a just-in-time manner.

This just-in-time prioritization concept is true even if you are running what you assume to be a stable project. As you finish some project requirements, you will have gained knowledge about the problem domain. You will have gained that knowledge both through your own analysis and development efforts, but also through the feedback you get from regularly scheduled reviews with your customers. This newfound knowledge is bound to result in changes in your to your backlog—which, again, would warrant a just-in-time approach to the prioritization of work.

Just-in-time Commitment

Once prioritized and placed on the Kanban board, there is also an explicit understanding that the new work items are now committed to. In a pull system, work is not "committed to" when it is placed in the backlog! It is only committed to in a just-in-time manner as determined by the team's explicit capacity.

But what do I mean by the word "commitment"? First, I mean commitment with a small "c". There should be no severe penalty for missing a commitment. No one should get fired. No one should lose their bonus or be denied a pay raise. But make no mistake. I do mean commitment. Once agreed to, I do mean that the team should do everything in its power to meet its commitments.

Second, commitment means that there is an expectation that, once started, an item will flow all the way through the process until completion. In other words, there is a commitment that flow will be conserved.

Lastly, commitment means communicating to our customers a Cycle Time range and probability for the committed-to item. Remember that once we commit to start work, the customer's first question will be "When is it going to be done?" This point of commitment is when we answer that question.

Allow me to further explain the three aspects of commitment by way of example. The placement of a work item in the Ready column means that the item has been both prioritized and committed to. This commitment means that all reasonable effort will be undertaken to make sure the item will flow all the way through the process to completion (just like in the sky diving example). It also means that a communication will be made to our customers regarding how long it should reasonably take that particular item to complete. That communication should take the form of "we expect this item to flow all the way through the process and exit in 14 days or less with an 85% probability of success". Many of you will recognize this as the language of "Service Level Agreements" or SLAs in Kanban. More on just what exactly SLAs are and how to set them for your process can be found in Chapter 12.

Not to get too off-topic here, but I hope this dispels another common myth I hear about flow-based systems, and in particular, Kanban. I often hear, "Kanban cannot work because there are no commitments". Nothing could be further from the truth. It is just that the approach to commitments is very different than, say, Scrum. Scrum commitments are made at the sprint level. At the beginning of a sprint, a team commits to getting some number of stories finished by the end of the sprint. That commitment is based more on upfront estimation and planning. In a flow-based approach, teams commit at the individual work item level. Once an item is pulled into the process a commitment is made as to when that item should be done. That commitment is based more on measurement and observation rather than planning and estimation. The point here is not to denigrate Scrum, but to get you to think about— especially if you are using a method like Scrum—how you might incorporate more flow-based principles into your current process.

Exceptions to Conservation of Flow

As with all of these "rules", there are always exceptions. There might be—and probably are—perfectly good reasons to discard work that is only partially completed. Maybe we have gained some knowledge that makes continuing to work on these particular items unnecessary, duplicative, or otherwise wasteful. Well, obviously, in those circumstances it makes perfect sense to abandon that work. When this happens, though, we should challenge ourselves with the following questions: "Why did that happen?" "Was there something that we could have done further upstream in our process to help avoid this situation?"

But, potentially more importantly, when these exceptions occur it is absolutely necessary to account for them properly in your data. Instead of just removing (or deleting) an item from your board never to be tracked again, it is probably best to mark that item as "finished" (whatever that means in your context), mark the date it was done, and then tag it with some attribute like "abandoned" or "discarded". In that way, we will be able to filter on that attribute later. You'll remember that I have spoken many times before about segmenting WIP based on different types. Well, one of those types might be work that has completed normally or not.

For example, let's say we have a board that looks like Figure 8.1. Let's further say that we start some work item and get it all the way to the "Development" column before we decide we do not need this particular functionality. In this case, the item should immediately be moved to the "Deployed" column, the current date should be captured, and the item should be tagged as "abandoned"—or with whatever other descriptor you choose to use.

Annotating an item in this way gives us several options when we go to generate our analytics later. You can imagine that we may want to generate several different views of a CFD for our exception cases. We may want to see all data together, we may want to only see items that have finished normally, or we may want to just see those items that were abandoned. Further, by accounting for these abandoned work items in this way, not only have we not violated the principle of the CoF, but we can also guarantee that we will be able to generate a valid CFD for all of those views.

A violation of the principle of conservation of flow should be treated as an opportunity for learning. Hopefully, your new-found understanding of this principle helps you to more readily recognize these learning opportunities and is yet another tool for you in your toolbox of continuous process improvement for predictability.

Conditioning Flow and Predictability

I just mentioned that part of the definition of commitment is that a team should do everything in its power to assure that once started an item completes and it completes in the timeframe that has been communicated to the customer. "Everything in its power" means first choosing a Cycle Time range and probability that is achievable. It also means doing what we can to choose items that have the best chance of meeting that goal. This idea of selecting items for success is a concept that I like to refer to as "Conditioning Flow".

Let me give you a few examples. Let's say that we are operating a process that is currently overloaded in Test. Let's further say that the next highest priority item that we wish to pull in off the backlog (though it has not been pulled in yet!) has a large amount of testing effort associated with it. But the second highest priority item has little to no testing effort associated with it. All other things being equal, we should probably pull the second priority in preference to the first priority. That is the concept of conditioning flow.

There are several other examples of this. Let's say the next highest priority to be pulled off the backlog requires a specific resource, but we know that that particular resource is going to be going on vacation for several weeks starting in two days. Obviously it wouldn't make sense to pull that item in, work on it for two days, and then block it while our expert is on vacation.

One last example might be that the team is in disagreement about whether the next priority item is of the right size to come into the system (right-sizing of work items will be discussed in Chapter 12). That disagreement probably stems from some uncertainty around the work item so maybe what the team decides to do is spike the story and pull that spike in first (by "spike" I mean a work item—user story—that is used to drive out risk and uncertainty in another work item).

Remember, we have control over a lot of these decisions. Making the best choices in these circumstances is usually the difference between whether our process is predictable or not. Conversations around conditioning flow are among the most important as they speak to what items are committed to next. Because we are talking about commitments and predictability here, we want to make sure that we are setting ourselves up for success from the very first pull transaction. We want to do what we can to condition our flow.

Conclusion

Whether you realized it or not before now, every time you started a piece of work (be it a project, a feature, or story) but then later abandoned it you violated the principle of Conservation of Flow and thus impaired your predictability. If work flows only part way through the system and gets kicked out or discarded—for whatever reason—then any effort that was expended on the eliminated item immediately becomes waste. Taken to its logical conclusion, you can understand why a team might want to conserve flow as much as possible. If work is constantly started but never finished, if this partially completed work is constantly discarded in favor of starting new work, then the Cycle Time metrics are going be skewed, and the system you are operating becomes infinitely unpredictable.

Of course, we live in the real world and these things are going to happen. Some might argue—and I certainly would not debate them if they did—that it is even more waste to continue to work on an item once we have gained information that the item is no longer necessary. By all means trash that work in those instances. However, just remember to account for that action appropriately in your data. Taking the time to do the proper accounting will pay huge predictability dividends later.

The idea of matching the arrival rate of your system to its departure rate, and the idea of making sure that flow is conserved for all items that enter your system go a long way to stabilize what would otherwise be considered an unstable system. When we have taken these steps we can now start to have some confidence that the metrics we are collecting off of our system are more reflective of a team's true capability. However, doing these two things alone still does not guarantee that our system is completely stable. It is this underlying sense of system stability that we need in order to reach one of our ultimate goals—a goal that I keep harping on throughout this text: predictability.

For the final piece of our stabilization problem, we must borrow some ideas from someone who—like most great thinkers—was not truly appreciated in his time.

Key Learnings and Takeaways

- Little's Law assumption #2 says that all work that is started will eventually be completed and exit the process.

- The concept that no work gets lost or does not ever exit the process is the second half of a concept known as the Conservation of Flow.
- To set ourselves up properly so as not to violate CoF we need to implement a just-in-time prioritization and just-in-time commitment strategy (these strategies are direct consequences of putting in place a pull system).
- In knowledge work, commitment means two things:
  - That once committed to, work will flow all the way through our process to completion.
  - That part of the commitment is a communication of an expected Cycle Time range and probability for a given item to complete.
- To not violate the Conservation of Flow, we need to account properly for items that have started but later get abandoned.
- Another benefit of accounting properly for abandoned items is that we can later filter our analytics on that data and help guarantee that the charts are built correctly.
- Conditioning flow means being smart about what items to pull in next based on contextual information that we currently have.

Chapter 9 - Flow Debt

Hyman Minski may be the best economist that you have never heard of. Among other things, he is known for his work on classifying debtors based on the types of financing they used when taking on their debt. Minski's theory was that borrowers could be categorized into one of three groups: hedge, speculative, and Ponzi. Hedge borrowers are those who can service both the principal and interest on their debt. Speculative borrowers can only pay the interest on their debt. And Ponzi borrowers have to constantly issue new debt in order to service the old.

Why am I telling you all this? To answer that question we must return to our old friend, the CFD. Specifically, recall CFD Property #4:

 CFD Property #4: The horizontal distance between any two lines on a CFD represents the Approximate Average Cycle Time for items that finished between the two workflow steps represented by the chosen two lines.

When you first read that, I am sure that most of you were thinking (and maybe still are) that being able to calculate only an *Approximate* Average Cycle Time was absolutely worthless. After all, why would you ever waste time measuring an Approximate Average Cycle Time from a CFD when you can just go and directly compute an *exact* Average Cycle Time from the chart's real, underlying data?

While those are good questions, I would argue that knowing the CFD's Approximate Average Cycle Time is extremely valuable. To understand why, we must revisit Little's Law Assumption #4:

 Little's Law Assumption #4: For the time period under consideration, the average age of WIP should neither be increasing nor decreasing.

The Approximate Average Cycle Time as predicted by the CFD can be compared to the exact Average Cycle Time as calculated from the very data used to build the CFD to begin with. The comparison of these two numbers will tell us if we can expect our exact Average Cycle Time to grow, decline, or stay the same over time. If our exact Average Cycle Time is either growing or declining then we have a violation of Little's Law assumption #4 which means that our predictability is in jeopardy.

So what are the scenarios we need to consider when comparing Approximate Average Cycle Time to exact Average Cycle Time? It turns out there are three. Those scenarios are:

1. The Approximate Average Cycle Time is *greater than* your actual Average Cycle Time.
2. The Approximate Average Cycle Time is *less than* your actual Average Cycle Time.
3. The Approximate Average Cycle Time is *roughly equal to* your actual Cycle Time.

It may sound trite, but an easy way to remember which of these is best is "scenario three is where you want to be." But it is because both scenarios one and two put predictability at risk that we will begin our discussion with those.

Approximate Average Greater Than Actual Average

If the Approximate Average Cycle Time is greater than the exact Average Cycle Time, then you can conclude that your process is incurring what I would call "Flow Debt".

 Flow Debt is when Cycle Time is artificially reduced for some items of Work In Progress by "borrowing" Cycle Time from other items of work in progress.

To explain, a smaller exact Average Cycle Time calculation when compared to the approximate average would tell you that you have (either explicitly or implicitly) favored the faster completion of some work items over the regular completion of others. You were not able to conjure that shortened Cycle Time out of thin air (we are not like the Fed who can just print money). This new ability to complete some items faster than they normally would have finished must have come from somewhere. What you did—whether you knew it or not—was to borrow Cycle Time from other work items that were already in progress. What you did was to create Flow Debt. This debt was used to pay for the expedited completion of the preferential work.

One great example of a process taking on Flow Debt is when a system has been designed with an expedite lane. A simple example of what an expedite lane looks like on a Kanban board is shown in Figure 9.1:

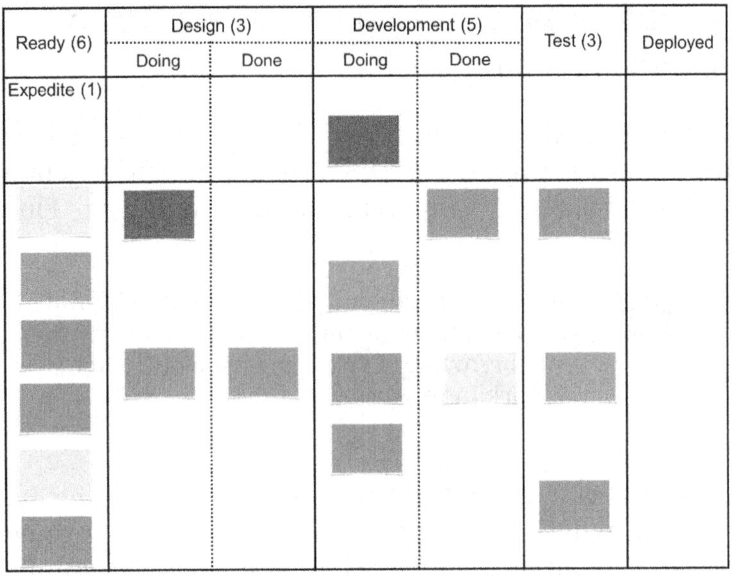

Figure 9.1: Expedite Lane Example

When used, most expedite lanes have an extremely low WIP limit on them (often set to one). Policies are also usually put in place such that items in expedite lanes can violate WIP limits at each step in the workflow. Further, most systems are designed such that when an expedite item is introduced, it is pulled immediately for work—it is allowed to "jump the queue" ahead of other work that is also ready to be pulled. If no resources are available to immediately pull the expedited entity, then many teams will block other items to free up team members to go act on the expedited work. Given these normal policies, you can see why it is so important to be extremely conservative when setting the WIP limit on an expedite lane (more information about expedited items, pull policies, and their effect on predictability, please see Chapter 13).

Looking at Figure 9.1, you will notice that the WIP

Limit for the expedite lane is indeed set to one. This means that only one work item can be in progress in that whole lane at any given time (but that work item can be anywhere in the lane: Ready, Design, Development, or Test). As you can also see, the expedite WIP limit has been adhered to and that the expedite item is in the Development column. Let's assume for a minute that no developers were available when this item was pulled into the Development step. What might happen is that the team would choose to block one (or more) of those other three items in progress in order to free up resources to go work on the expedited ticket. The team has chosen to take the time that was to be allocated for work that was already in progress and apply that time to the expedited item. What has happened is that the team has chosen to artificially age one item (or more) in order to shorten the Cycle Time of another. This is a classic example of the creation of Flow Debt.

The problem is that this debt must be repaid (think the Mafia here and not the U.S. Government). The payment of this debt will come in one of two ways:

1. The work items that were "passed over" in deference to the expedite items will eventually themselves complete (in accordance with the principle of Conservation of Flow). When they do complete their Cycle Times will be much longer than they normally would have been because they were forced to artificially age. Thus, debt repayment comes in the form of longer Cycle Times for items already in progress. The resulting consequence is that you can have no confidence in the "average" Cycle Time you thought you were capable of because the metrics you had collected did not include this debt. You can have no confidence in this aver-

age because the accumulation of debt has made it invalid; or,

2. The work items that were "passed over" will be eventually kicked out of the system because they are no longer considered valuable (in violation of Conservation of Flow); i.e., the window of time to realize their value has passed. When these items are thrown out of your process, any effort or time that has been spent on progressing them through the system immediately becomes waste. Thus, the payment of Flow Debt is the wasted effort that could have been spent in realizing the value of the discarded work item or in the form of wasted effort that could have been spent realizing the value of something else.

Either way, Flow Debt is repaid in the form of less predictability for your process.

I do not want you to conclude that all Flow Debt is bad. What you need to do is simply recognize that your system is incurring debt. The challenge for you, then, is to think about how you might categorize your borrowing into one of Minski's types: Hedge, Speculative, or Ponzi.

To classify what type of debtor you might be, ask yourself the following questions:

1. Hedge: Are expedites in your process more the exception than the rule (that is to say, does your board not have expedites significantly more often that it does have expedites)? When you do have expedited requests, do you truly only ever have one item (or some WIP limited amount of expedited items) in your process at a time? Does this time with no expedited items give you an opportunity

to finish work that was otherwise blocked for previously expedited items? When you get an expedited item, are you allowed to finish existing work before the expedite is picked up? If the answers to these questions is yes, then you are probably running a properly "hedged" system.

2. Speculative: Is there always at least one item in your process and never a time when you are not working on expedited work of some kind? Do you routinely violate your expedited item WIP limit? If the answers to these questions is yes, then you are probably running a speculative system and you might want to explore some options to apply more rigor to your expedite process.

3. Ponzi. Is all the work you do considered an expedite? Do expedited items take up all of your available capacity such that you never get a chance to work on more "normal" items? Are your pull criteria based not on explicit policies but on whomever is screaming the loudest? If the answer to these questions is yes, then what you are really running is a process Ponzi scheme. You will never be able to repay the debt you have accumulated and any notion of total process predictability is gone. You are fooling yourself if you continue to start "normal" work in addition to expedited work in this world. That normal work will almost never complete, or it will swapped out for other work, or it will finish far too late for anyone to care. In my mind, this is the antithesis of flow.

I want to make sure that you know that I am not advocating that you spend a lot of time on this classification nor that you become an expert in economic theory. What I do want you to ask yourself is are you able to repay the debt that you are taking out? How much debt is reasonable in your context? I guarantee that there are going to be some very good reasons to take on "Hedge" Flow Debt from time to time (a great analogy to this in the real world is when prospective homeowners take out a mortgage—assuming they can be repaid, most mortgages are considered good debt). The question for you becomes: are you able to service the Flow Debt that you have taken out?

By the way, I have picked on expedite work items here, but it should be noted that an explicit expedite lane is not the only way to incur Flow Debt.

Extending the scenario from above, let's say that you have an item in the "Design Done" column. And let's say that that item just sits there and never gets pulled into "Development Doing" because you care constantly choosing to pull other items in preference to it. If so, then congratulations, you have Flow Debt.

This particular scenario is depicted in the following diagram (Figure 9.2):

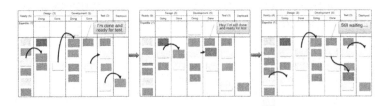

Figure 9.2: Ignoring an Item While it is Queuing

Another example of the creation of Flow Debt might be if you have blocked items that you ignore or do not actively work to get unblocked and moving again as quickly as possible (Figure 9.3):

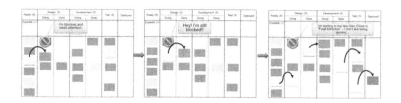

Figure 9.3: Ignoring a Blocked Item

I am sure there are other examples, but I will leave it as an exercise for the reader to identify the types of Flow Debt in your context.

By the way, the concepts in this chapter can be applied to any type of debt that you may incur in your process (e.g., technical debt). The trick is to recognize that you are creating debt and have a constructive conversation about how that debt is going to be repaid.

Approximate Average is Less Than Actual Average

This scenario is a bit less interesting than the last one. If in the above situation we were talking about accumulating Flow Debt, then the case where the Approximate Average Cycle Time on your CFD is less than your actual Average Cycle Time means that you are paying off Flow Debt (again, for the time interval under consideration).

A larger actual Average Cycle Time means that those items that have—for whatever reason—languished in progress are now finally completing. The actual average has become inflated because as the artificially aged items complete they make the actual average calculation come out "larger" than it otherwise would have been under normal circumstances.

However, paying off Flow Debt also hampers predictability. Items that finish with large amounts of Flow Debt attached to them skew Cycle Time numbers. An increased variability in Cycle Time means that we must communicate a larger range for the SLA of our process (see the discussion in the previous chapter and in Chapter 12). A good analogy of why this might be dangerous is that of a restaurant who has customers waiting to be seated. Imagine that the true wait time for customers is fifteen minutes, but because of variability in their seating process, the restaurant has to communicate a two hour wait time to arriving patrons. What do you think those customers will do? The same thing will happen in your own process. The more your system is unpredictable, the more your customers will begin to look elsewhere for service.

Remember that these conclusions can only be drawn assuming we are running an otherwise stable system (i.e., nothing about the underlying system design has changed materially).

Approximate Average Roughly Equal to Actual Average

This case is where you want to be most of the time. If your Approximate Average Cycle Time is approximately equal to your actual Average Cycle Time, then your process is probably performing in a fairly orderly, predictable manner. You are not overloaded with expedite requests, you are not allowing items to stay blocked indefinitely, and you are not allowing items to queue arbitrarily. In other words, you are neither accumulating nor repaying Flow Debt.

That is not to suggest that there are not any other areas of your process that are unhealthy. And if you do find yourself in this situation, do not pat yourself on the back too quickly. A more stable system such as the one that you have just engineered requires constant vigilance against the multitude of destabilizing forces that present themselves every day.

How Different is Different?

So how different do my different average calculations need to be in order for me to take action? Like most questions in Kanban, the answer to this one is, "it depends". The conclusions you draw and the actions you should take are highly context specific.

One reason this question is difficult to answer is because the Approximate Average Cycle Time calculation is just that: an approximation. Therefore, some difference between the approximate and the actual is to be expected. If the difference is about 10%, then you might not get too excited. However, if the difference is 50%, then that might be a pretty good clue to take action. Over time you will get a very good feel for what constitutes "different" in your world.

Conclusion

Are you running a process Ponzi scheme? Do you even know?

If your process is unpredictable, one of the first places to investigate is how much Flow Debt you are carrying. Think about what process policies you can put in place to restore some stability to your system. If you believe your system is not "ponz-ified", what process policies can you institute to ensure that your process remains stable?

Lastly, I want to say that I have tried very hard to

steer clear of using the term "Class of Service" (CoS) in this chapter. Many of you will have figured out, however, that CoS is exactly what I am talking about. I personally am not a big fan of the way CoS is normally touted in our Lean/Agile/Kanban community. To be clear, I am not a fan not because CoS is inherently bad, but because most teams do not know how to implement it properly—nor do they understand what this improper implementation is doing to their system's predictability, performance, and/or risk management ability. Those three goals, ironically, are usually the exact ones promoted to justify the use of CoS.

Unfortunately, a deeper discussion of CoS and its perils will have to wait until Chapter 13. That is because I need to move on to the more pressing need of introducing the next of our flow analytics: the Cycle Time Scatterplot.

Key Learnings and Takeaways

- Flow Debt is when Cycle Time is artificially reduced for some work items in progress by "borrowing" Cycle Time from other work items in progress.
- Some examples of scenarios that lead to the creation of Flow Debt are:
  - Classes of Service
  - Blockers
  - Other order of pull policies in place (whether they are explicit or not)
- Comparing the Approximate Average Cycle Time for work items on a CFD with the exact Average Cycle Time for those work items (calculated from the data) can give us an idea of whether Flow Debt is being created or not.

- When the Approximate Average Cycle Time on your CFD is *greater than* your actual Average Cycle Time then your process is accumulating Flow Debt.
- When the Approximate Average Cycle Time is *less than* your actual Average Cycle Time then your process is paying off Flow Debt.
- When the Approximate Average Cycle Time is *roughly equal to* your actual Cycle Time then your process is stable from a Flow Debt perspective.
- Flow Debt leads to process unpredictability because by Little's Law Assumption #2 the work items that were allowed to artificially age eventually will need to complete and leave the system. This artificial aging leads not only to longer overall Cycle Times, but more variability in your Cycle Time data.

PART THREE - CYCLE TIME SCATTERPLOTS FOR PREDICTABILITY

Chapter 10 - Introduction to Cycle Time Scatterplots

I spent a lot of time in the last several chapters talking about how Cumulative Flow Diagrams can give you a good idea of how long it takes for items to flow through your process *on average*. However, there are going to be times when doing analysis based solely on average is not going to be good enough (things like forecasting a completion date come to mind, for example). Not to worry because we can do much better than analysis based on averages anyway. This is where Scatterplots come in.

Scatterplots are a little less complicated than Cumulative Flow Diagrams but that in no way diminishes their usefulness. What diminishes their usefulness is, again, the misinformation and disinformation that has been published about them. In fact, my guess is that until now you have probably not come across the term "Scatterplot" in reference to Cycle Time analysis. Rather, you have probably been told that you need to look at your Cycle Time data in something called a "Control Chart". Not true. I will talk about why Control Charts are really not all that useful in our domain a little later (please note that Statistical Process Control will not be covered at all in this book). For now do not get hung up on confusing terms like "Control Chart". There is a much simpler and better way.

But before I get into the explanation about how to do basic quantitative and qualitative analysis using Scatterplots, I need to make one thing clear about how to read this chapter. For this discussion I am going to focus only on how to chart the flow metric Cycle Time on a Scatterplot. In reality you can put pretty much any metric that you want to in a Scatterplot. You can put things like Throughput, bugs per feature, work items per epic, etc. For the purposes of this chapter, however, whenever I say the word "Scatterplot" without any qualifier, what I really mean is "Cycle Time Scatterplot" (if you would like a refresher on how I am choosing to define Cycle Time, then please revisit Chapter 2).

What is a Cycle Time Scatterplot?

Just as with the CFDs, it will first be beneficial to get a basic understanding of a Scatterplot's anatomy before diving into what these charts can tell us.

If you have never seen a Cycle Time Scatterplot before, then one is displayed in Figure 10.1 for your reference:

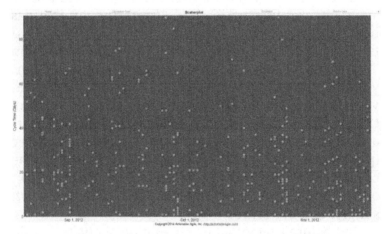

Figure 10.1: A Basic Cycle Time Scatterplot

As you can see from Figure 10.1, across the bottom

(the X-axis) is some representation of the progression of time. Like CFDs, the X-axis essentially represents a timeline for our process. The tick marks on the X-axis represents our choice of labels for that timeline. When labeling the X-axis, you can choose whatever frequency of labels you want. In this particular Scatterplot, we have chosen to label every month. However you can choose whatever label is best for your specific needs. You can choose to label every two weeks, every month, every day, etc.

I should point out that in Figure 10.1 I have chosen to show the timeline progression from left to right. This is not a requirement, it is only a preference. I could have easily shown time progression from right to left. I, personally, have never seen a Cycle Time Scatterplot that shows time progression from right to left, but there is no reason why one could not be constructed that way. However, for the rest of this chapter (and this book), I will show all Scatterplot time progressions from left to right.

Up the side (the Y-axis) of your chart is going to be some representation of Cycle Time. Again, you can choose whatever units of Cycle Time that you want for this axis. For example, you can measure Cycle Time in days, weeks, months, etc.

To generate a Scatterplot, any time a work item completes, you find the date that it completed across the bottom and plot a dot on the chart area according to its Cycle Time. For example, let's say a work item took seven days to complete and it finished January 1, 2013. On the Scatterplot you would go across the bottom to find January 1, 2013 and then go up and put it a dot at seven days. Recall that for CFDs you could choose whatever time reporting interval you wanted to plot your data. In a Scatterplot, however, there is really no concept of a reporting interval. A dot is always plotted on the day a given work item finishes.

Note that you could have several items that finish on same day with the same Cycle Time. In that case, you would simply plot the several dots on top of one another. Hopefully whatever tool you are using to plot your Scatterplot can handle this case, and, further, can alert you to the instances where you have several dots on top of each other. In the ActionableAgile™ Analytics tool, we signify this situation by putting a little number on the dot to show there is more than one work item located at that point (as also shown in Figure 10.1).

Over time as you plot more and more work item completions, a random set of dots will emerge on your chart. The original diagram I showed you in Figure 10.1 is a good example of what I am talking about. So how do we get useful information off of a chart that just looks like a bunch of random dots?

Percentile Lines

The first thing that we can do to gain a better understanding of our process's Cycle Time performance is to draw what I would call "standard percentile lines" on our Scatterplot. I should stress upfront that this standard percentile approach is only a starting point—you will have every opportunity to change these percentiles as you get a better understanding of your context. I would argue, however, that these standard percentiles represent a good enough place to start for most teams.

The best way to explain how to use standard percentiles on a Scatterplot is by example. I want to refer you again to the chart shown in Figure 10.1. Looking at this graph the first line that we could draw would be at the 50th percentile of Cycle Times. The 50th percentile line is going to represent the value for a Cycle Time such that if we draw a line completely across the chart at that Cycle Time, 50% of the dots on the chart fall below that line and 50% of the dots are above that line. This calculation is shown in Figure 10.2 below.

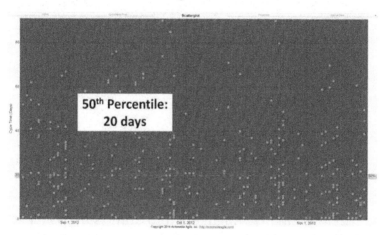

Figure 10.2: The 50th Percentile Line added to a Scatterplot

In this example the 50th percentile line occurs at twenty days. That means that 50% of the work items that have flowed through our process took twenty days or less to complete. Another way of saying that is that when a work item enters our process it has a 50% chance of finishing in twenty days or less (more on this concept a little later).

The next line that might be of interest to us is the 85th percentile. Again this line represents the amount of time it took for 85% of our work items to finish. In Figure 10.3 you can see that the 85th percentile line occurs at 43 days. That means that 85% of the dots on our chart fall below that line and 15% of the dots on our chart fall above that line. This percentile line tells us is that when a work item enters our process it has an 85% chance of finishing in 43 days or less. This calculation is shown in Figure 10.3 below.

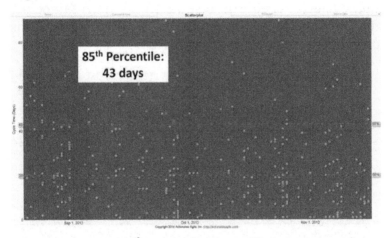

Figure 10.3: The 85th Percentile Line Added to a Scatterplot

Another line we might want to draw is the 95th percentile line. As before this line represents the amount of time at which 95% of our work items complete. In Figure 10.4 the 95th percentile line occurs at 63 days and tells us that our work items have a 95% chance of finishing in 63 days or less. This calculation is shown in Figure 10.4 below.

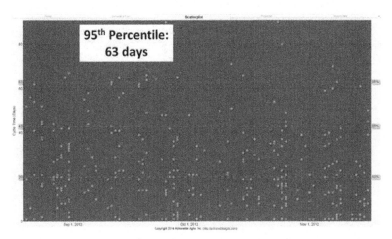

Figure 10.4: The 95th Percentile Line added to a Scatterplot

The 50th, 85th, and 95th percentiles are probably the most popular "standard" percentiles to draw. Other percentiles that you will see, though, could include the 30th and 70th. Calculating those percentiles is exactly the same as I have just demonstrated with the others. A Scatterplot with all of these percentile lines is shown in Figure 10.5 (note the 30th percentile is 11 days and the 70th percentile is 32 days):

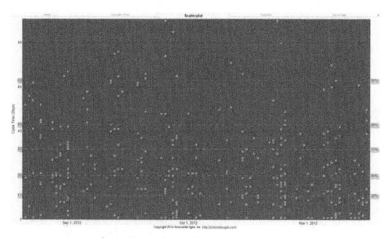

Figure 10.5: 30th, 50th, 70th, 85th, and 95th **Percentile Lines all shown on a Scatterplot**

I am sure you have noticed that as we increase our level of confidence we have to increase the amount of time it takes for work items to complete. This is due to the variability inherent in our process. We will spend a little bit of time talking about variability later in this chapter. What we will see in that discussion is that no matter how hard we try to drive it out, variability will always be present in our system. But that is okay. It turns out that we do need a little variability in order to protect flow. However, what we are going to want to understand is how much of that variability is self-imposed, and how much of that variability is outside of our control. The good news is that I will give you ways to identify each of these cases and strategies with which to handle them.

As I mentioned earlier, drawing these standard percentile lines is a good start, but you can see that you can easily add or subtract other percentile lines to your chart as you see fit. Which lines to draw is mostly going to be a function of what you want to learn from your data.

Your Data is Not Normal

Many electronic tools will draw arithmetic mean and standard deviation lines on their Scatterplots instead of drawing the standard percentile lines as described above. That is to say, these tools will figure out the arithmetic mean of all of their Cycle Time data and then first draw that horizontal line on the chart. They will then compute a standard deviation for that data and draw horizontal lines corresponding to the mean plus one standard deviation and the mean minus one standard deviation.

They might go further and draw the +2 standard deviation and -2 standard deviation lines as well as the +3 standard deviation and -3 standard deviation lines. They will call the top standard deviation line the "Upper Control Limit" (UCL) and they will call the bottom standard deviation line the "Lower Control Limit" (LCL). They will then call the resulting graph a "Control Chart". If you are using an electronic tool to track your process maybe you have seen an example of a Control Chart.

You might have further heard several claims about these charts. First you may have heard that on a Control Chart (as described above) 68.2% of the dots fall between the plus one standard deviation line and the minus one standard deviation line. They might further go on to say that over 99% of the dots fall between the +3 standard deviation in the -3 standard deviation line. You might have further heard that the reason you want to segment your data this way is because this type of visualization will be able to tell you if your process is in control or not (hence the name Control Chart). Any dots that fall above the UCL or below the LCL, it is argued, signify the points in your process that are out of control.

What is being called a Control Chart here is supposedly inspired by the work of Walter A. Shewhart while employed at Bell Labs in the 1920s. Shewhart's work was later picked up by W. Edwards Deming who became one of the biggest proponents of the Control Chart visualization.

There is only one problem. By using the method outlined above what they have created is most certainly not a Control Chart—at least not in the Shewhart tradition. What Shewhart Control Charts are and how to construct them are way beyond the scope of this book, but just know that you should be skeptical whenever you see someone show you something that is labeled "Control Chart"—as it most certainly is not. While I am a big fan of Shewhart's work, I am not convinced that canonical Shewhart Control Charts are applicable in a knowledge work world (I am not saying they are definitely not; I am just saying I have not yet been convinced).

As these things usually go, the problem is much worse than you might think. That tools vendors' charts are most assuredly not Control Charts notwithstanding, there still remains one (at least) fatal flaw with a pseudo Control Chart approach. These charts—especially the calculations for the UCLs and LCLs—assume that your data is normally distributed. I can all but guarantee you that your Cycle Time data is not and will not be normally distributed. We will talk briefly about how your data is distributed later (in Chapter 10a), but just know that for now the conclusions based on the standard deviation calculations above when applied to your non-normally distributed data will be incorrect.

The use of this normal distribution method is so pervasive because that is the type of statistics that that most of us are familiar with. One very important consequence of working in the knowledge work domain is that you pretty much have to forget any statistics training that you may have had up until this point (for a great book on why we need to forget the statistics that we have been taught read "The Flaw of Averages"). We do not live in a world of normal distributions. But as we are about to see with Scatterplots, that is not going to be a problem at all.

As a quick aside, you may have also heard the name "Run Chart" in association with these diagrams. Again, the Scatterplots I am talking about here are not Run Charts. A deep discussion of Run Charts is also beyond the scope of this book. I am not saying that Run Charts are not useful, by the way—far from it. I am just trying to be clear that this chapter's Cycle Time Scatterplots are most certainly not Run Charts.

Getting back to standard percentiles, there are at least three reasons why I like those lines better than the dubious Control Chart tactic mentioned above. First, notice that when I described how to draw the standard percentile lines on a Scatterplot I never made one mention of how the underlying Cycle Time data might be distributed. And that is the beauty of it. To draw those lines I do not need to know how your data is distributed. In fact, I do not care (yet). These percentile line calculations work regardless of the underlying distribution.

Second, note how simple the calculations are. You just count up all the dots and multiply by percentages. Simple. You are not required to have an advanced degree in statistics in order to draw these lines.

Third, percentiles are not skewed by outliers. One of the great disadvantages of a mean and standard deviation approach (other than the false assumption of normally distributed data) is that both of those statistics are heavily influenced by outliers. You have probably heard the saying, "If Bill Gates walks into a bar, then on average everyone in the bar is a millionaire". Obviously, in the Bill Gates example, average is no longer a useful statistic. The same type of phenomenon happens in our world. However, when you do get those extreme Cycle Time outliers, your percentile lines will not budge all that much. It is this robustness in the face of outliers that is why percentile lines are generally better statistics for the analysis of Cycle Time.

As I mentioned at the beginning of this section, chances are if you are using an electronic tool for metrics that it will not show you a Scatterplot view with percentile lines overlaid. So what are you to do? You can use a tool like excel and generate the charts yourself. Or you can use the ActionableAgile™ Analytics tool as it takes care of everything for you.

Conclusion

Randomness exists in all processes. One of the best ways to visualize the randomness in your process is to put your Cycle Time data into a Scatterplot. As with CFDs, a Cycle Time Scatterplot can yield vast amounts of quantitative information (the qualitative side of Scatterplots will be discussed in Chapter 11).

I mentioned at the beginning of this chapter that Cycle Time Scatterplots are a great way to visualize Cycle Time data that goes far beyond simple analysis by average. I hope that you are convinced of that now.

I have only scratched the surface so far with regard to the quantitative analysis of Scatterplots, but this should be enough to get you started. It is enough, in fact, to allow us to switch gears and look at how qualitative analysis of these charts might work.

However, before we get into the details of how to interpret Scatterplots, I would like to take a short detour to discuss how to view the shape of your Cycle Time data.

Key Learnings and Takeaways

- Scatterplots are one of the best analytics for visualizing Cycle Time data.
- This type of visualization communicates a lot of quantitative and qualitative information at a glance.
- The anatomy of a Scatterplot is:
  - The X-axis represents the process timeline.
  - The Y-axis represents the Cycle Time for an item to complete.
  - The labels and reporting intervals on the chart are at the sole discretion of the graph's creator.
- A Cycle Time Scatterplot is not a Control Chart. It is not a Run Chart, either.
- One of the best ways to put some structure around Cycle Time Scatterplot data is to draw percentile lines. Consider starting with the 50th, 70th, 85th, and 95th percentiles.
- Percentiles have the advantages of being easy to calculate, being agnostic of the underlying data distribution, and not being skewed by outliers.

Chapter 10a - Cycle Time Histograms

While the analysis of Cycle Time Histograms is technically an advanced topic, I do want to discuss them briefly in the interest of completeness. The good news is that you need not master this analysis to be successful with the predictability concepts presented in this book.

So why even mention Histograms at all? I mention them here for two reasons. First, Histograms are closely related to Cycle Time Scatterplots in that they are really just another view of the same data shown on a Scatterplot. And, second, a brief introduction to Histograms will be helpful for other concepts I will introduce later (e.g., Classes of Service and Forecasting).

As I have done so many times previously, I need to insert a disclaimer at this point. For the purposes of this chapter whenever I say the word "Histogram" without any qualifier, what I really mean is "Cycle Time Histogram". Further, this chapter is not meant to represent an exhaustive treatment of these charts. For that I invite you to explore some of the books listed in the Bibliography at the end of this book.

What is a Histogram?

Simply stated, a Histogram is graphical display of data that uses bars of different heights to show the frequency of different data points within an overall dataset. A Histogram is very similar to a bar chart with one important distinction being that a Histogram groups population elements together in ranges. An example Histogram is shown in Figure 10a.1:

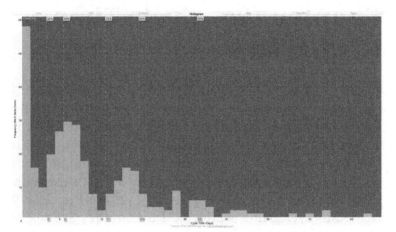

Figure 10a.1: An Example Cycle Time Histogram

Figure 10a.1 shows frequency on the vertical (or Y) axis and Cycle Times on the horizontal (or X) axis. The advantage of this chart is that it gives you an overall idea of the shape of the distribution of your underlying data. Knowing this shape can give you some insight to the problem areas of your process. You might be interested to know that in knowledge work, a Histogram that shows Cycle Time usually looks much like what is shown in Figure 10a.1. That is to say Histograms in our world usually have a big hump on the left and a long tail to the right. Why this type of shape occurs in knowledge work, whether it is a log-normal or a Weibull or some other distribution, and what the shape is telling us are questions that have answers that are beyond the scope of this introductory book. Just know that a deep analysis is possible (and potentially very powerful).

Constructing a Histogram

Constructing a Histogram is rather straightforward. As I just mentioned, the vertical axis of this chart is frequency and the horizontal axis represents the ranges of intervals (or bins) that you are interested in. For a given data population, you go through each element and every time a given data point falls within a particular range, you increment the frequency of bin. The height of the bins, therefore, represents the number of times that data points of your dataset occurs within that range.

To illustrate, let's consider the example of rolling four independent (but equal) six-sided dice. In this example we will add up the face value on the dice after each roll and plot them on a Histogram. The bins that we will use for the horizontal axis will therefore be all the possible values for a given roll. That is, since the smallest value for a given roll is four (four times one), our bins will start at four. Since the highest possible value is twenty-four (four times six), then our bins will end at twenty-four. We will have one bin for each possible value between four and twenty four. Figure 10a.2 shows the Histogram after ten, one hundred, and five thousand rolls, respectively (please note that these Histograms were not generated with the ActionableAgile™ Analytics tool).

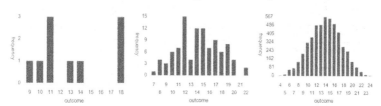

Figure 10a.2: Rolling Dice Histogram (10 trials, 100 trials, and 5000 trials, respectively)

The thing to note about Figure 10a.2 is that as the

number of trials increases, the shape of the distribution sharpens. In other words, more data is usually better than less data when it comes to visualization (but do not be fooled into thinking you need massive amounts of data to be successful with a statistical approach).

Just like the experiment of adding up the results of rolling four, equal, six-sided dice produced random results that could be plotted as the Histograms shown in Figure 10a.2, so your process will generate random Cycle Times that can be displayed in a similar manner. Figure 10a.1 is one such example. Again, the lesson here is that the more data you have, the sharper the picture you get.

As I said in the introduction, a Histogram is simply another way to plot the data contained with the Scatterplot. As such, we can place percentile lines on them in much the same way that was explained in Chapter 10. Figure 10a.1 shows an example of this.

Having both views with the same percentiles is useful because both views serve different purposes. The Scatterplot is a temporal view of data that can show trends of dots over time. A Histogram is a condensed, spatial view based on the frequency of occurrence of Cycle Times. Looking at the Scatterplot in Figure 10.1 it may not be obvious that the shape of the data is that in Figure 10a.1. Likewise, looking at the Figure in 10a.1 you may not be able to detect any patterns of Cycle Times over a given timeline.

Conclusion

Though short, my hope is that this chapter has given you some insight as to why you might want to look at your Cycle Time data in the analytical chart known as a Histogram. I took this detour as I wanted to make sure you had this introduction given that I am going to leverage these charts to explain key concepts in the following chapters.

Now that we have checked Histograms off of our list, it is time to get back to the more pressing matter of how to interpret the data displayed in a Scatterplot.

Key Learnings and Takeaways

- A Histogram is a graphical display of data that uses bars of different heights to show the frequency of different data points within an overall dataset.
- The Histogram is a condensed, spatial view that shows the shape of the underlying Cycle Time data while the Scatterplot is a temporal view of data that can show trends of dots over time.
- Histograms can be used for more advanced Cycle Time analysis and forecast modeling techniques.

Chapter 11 - Interpreting Cycle Time Scatterplots

One of the great advantages of a Scatterplot is that it allows us to visually detect trends in our process's Cycle Time over time.

But before we get started, I want to expressly callout the maxim that I have repeated over and over until now:

 Your policies shape your data and your data shape your policies.

I mention this again because as you read through the explanations of some of the Scatterplot patterns that follow, you will quickly realize that most of these results are due to policies that are explicitly under the team's control. If you see some anomalies creep into your data, then the first thing you should ask yourself is "What policy (either explicit or implicit) do we have in place that is causing our data to look like this?" Use that data to suggest changes to process policies and then verify the change had the intended effect by further collecting and re-examining future data.

The rest of this chapter will be devoted to taking a closer look at some of the trends and patterns that may appear on your Cycle Time Scatterplot.

The Triangle

A triangle-shaped pattern as shown in Figure 11.1 will appear in any situation where Cycle Time increases over time.

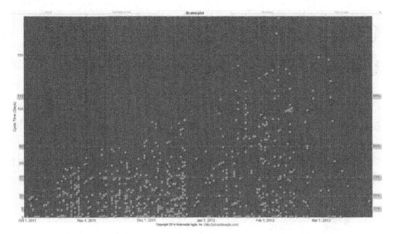

Figure 11.1: A Triangle Pattern on a Scatterplot

Notice how the dots in the above Scatterplot (Figure 11.1) form a pattern that looks something like a triangle. Explaining this phenomenon is going to require us to review the fundamental property of Scatterplots: dots do not actually show up until a work item has finished. The items that have longer Cycle Times are going to need an extended period before they appear on the chart. That means that the longer the Cycle Time (the dot's Y-component) the longer the amount of time we are going to have to wait (the dot's X-component) to see that data point.

There are two major cases to consider whenever you see this pattern emerge on your Scatterplot. The first is when arrivals exceed departures, and the second is the accumulation of Flow Debt.

For the first major case, let's consider the context where a project starts from zero WIP. Whenever you start with an empty process it is going to take time to "prime the pump". Obviously, in those early stages work will be pulled in faster than it departs—even if we are limiting WIP. We are going to need time for each workflow step to fill up to its capacity and get a predictable flow going. Once that stable flow occurs, then the expectation is that the triangle will eventually flatten out into a more predictable arrangement.

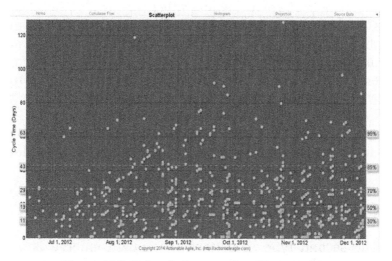

Figure 11.2: Triangle Pattern that Flattens Out

In Figure 11.2 you can see how the dots form a triangle up until about the beginning of September, but then flatten out as the process stabilizes.

If you have the case where WIP never gets to zero, then a triangle will form whenever you have a non-trivial period of time where the top line and bottom line on your CFD diverge (see Figure 7.5). The pattern in Figure 11.1 could be due to the fact that for almost the whole timeline of the process represented here, this team did not control WIP. As we have said over and over in previous chapters, increased WIP leads to increased Cycle Times. Not controlling WIP will only cause Cycle Times to get longer and longer and longer.

The second major reason that a triangle pattern might emerge on your Scatterplot is a process that is dominated by Flow Debt. Remember from Chapter 9 that Flow Debt accrues any time that items are left to age arbitrarily. Aging of items could be due to blocks, too much WIP (as in the case above), or poor (or misunderstood) pull policies. Even if a team explicitly controls WIP, Flow Debt can occur. Flow Debt can therefore easily explain the emergence of a triangle. The items at the bottom of the triangle were those items that were pulled preferentially through the process (for whatever reason) whereas items toward the top of the triangle were left to age unnecessarily (again, for whatever reason). If Arrival Rate and Departure Rate are matched, then the only way you will not see a triangle on your Scatterplot is if you control Flow Debt.

Clusters of Dots

The second type of pattern that might emerge is an obvious clustering of dots on your Scatterplot. Consider, for example, the following chart in Figure 11.3:

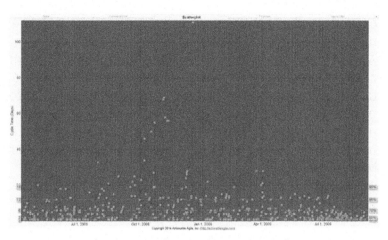

Figure 11.3: Clusters on a Scatterplot

Note the clusters of dots at the beginning of October 2008 (around the middle of Figure 11.3) and at the end of July 2009 (the lower right side of Figure 11.3). As with all of these analytics, the point is to get to the point where you can ask the right questions sooner. So, when we see clusters of dots like in Figure 8.11, we are at the very least going to want to ask "what's going on here?" That should probably quickly be followed by "is this a good thing or a bad thing?" If it is bad, what can we do about it?

By the way, not all clusters of very low Cycle Times are good. Look at the cluster of dots for July 2009 again in Figure 8.11. What do you think might be causing our Cycle Times to have decreased so radically? Are you only thinking of good reasons? What might be some bad reasons that would cause this to happen? One sinister reason that I see all too often is mandatory overtime. It stands to reason that if your normal data is based on 8 hour days and 5 day work weeks that moving to 12 hour days and 7 day work weeks will probably make your Cycle Time look better (assuming, of course, that you continue to limit WIP!). But is that a good thing? I know most managers would say yes. I would say otherwise. And from a predictability perspective, it is terrible. Not only are long periods of mandatory overtime not sustainable but it also skews our data. Do you really want to be offering an SLA or making a forecast with mandatory overtime as one of the upfront assumptions that is baked in? If your answer to that question is "yes", then this book is not for you.

Gaps

Gaps in the dots on your Scatterplot means that no work items finished in that particular time interval. These gaps will directly correlate with the same time period that a flat section appears on the bottom line of your CFD. Flat lines on the CFD mean nothing completed; if nothing has completed then no dots will show up on your Scatterplot. Further, the cause of these gaps is the same reasons that CFD Throughput flattens out: public holidays, external blockers, batch transfer, etc.

Batch transfer bears some more exploration. It is not uncommon for a Scrum team to generate a Scatterplot that looks like Figure 11.4:

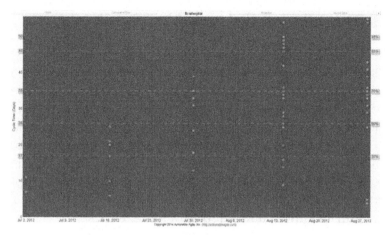

Figure 11.4: Batch Transfer on a Scatterplot

The stacks of dots that you see here are at the sprint boundaries when there is a mad rush to complete work items. But look at how the data thins out between those stacks. Is this a good thing or a bad thing? Either way, what impact is this having on our predictability? If you think it is a bad thing, what might you do change that?

You might be surprised that I have not talked much about variation in this chapter. The truth is that I am not going to talk all that much about variation here. A full treatment of variation is well beyond the scope of this book (and has already been accomplished by much greater minds than mine). Further, understanding variation is more of a "thinking" thing rather than a "tool" thing. I believe that it is mostly impossible to classify variation of your data into things like "special causes" or "common causes" simply by looking at a Scatterplot (at least as I have described them here). Rather, my only two immediate goals are (1) to discuss some patterns that may appear on your Scatterplot, and (2) to get you to start asking some questions about why those patterns may have emerged.

Internal and External Variability

I began this chapter by suggesting that a Scatterplot just looks like a random collection of dots on a chart. The reason that Scatterplots look the way they do is because of the variation that exists in your process. The first thing to know about variation is that it will always exist. From a predictability perspective, the point is not to always try to drive variation out; rather, the point will be to understand the causes of that variation in an attempt to make your process more predictable.

For example, take a look at Figure 11.5:

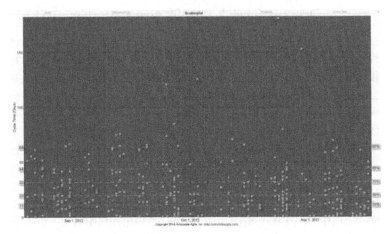

Figure 11.5: An Example Scatterplot

At first glance you might be inclined to dismiss those dots at the top of the Scatterplot as outliers. You might question the value of including them since they are clearly one-offs. You might even (if you did not like yourself very much) do some further quantitative analysis to prove that those dots are not statistically significant. And you know what, if you made those assertions then I probably would not argue with you too strenuously. I would say, though, that while those points are outliers, they obviously happened and probably warrant some deeper investigation. I would also say that, while potentially statistically insignificant, there might be some good contextual or qualitative reasons to keep them in from an analysis perspective.

To illustrate this point, consider what the chart in Figure 11.5 is communicating to us. The 50th percentile of Cycle Time is 20 days and the 85th percentile is 44 days. But you can see there is a work item on this chart that took 181 days! Can you think of some reasons that would have caused that particular work item to take so long? Maybe the team had a development dependency on an external vendor or a dependency on some other internal development team. Maybe the team did not have a test environment immediately available to them. Maybe the customer was not immediately available for sign-off. The shared theme for all of these reasons is that those work items took so long to complete due to reasons outside of the team's control. And that is generally what you will find as you move "up the stack" of dots on a Scatterplot. More often than not, those outliers will be caused by circumstances that are outside of the team's control.

The opposite is also generally true. As you move "down the stack" the work items that took less time to complete were generally due to reasons that were totally under the team's control. For example, reconsider that work item that I just mentioned that took 181 days to complete. Do you really think that item would have taken 181 days if it was totally under control of the team that was working on it? Maybe, but probably not. Additionally, look at those dots that just barely violated that 85th percentile line. Do you think that there were things that the team could have done to ensure that the violation did not happen? Probably (swarm or break up the item are two ideas that come immediately to mind).

I hope that you are getting a feel for the type of variability analysis that I am asking you to perform with these Scatterplots. Will all outliers be due to external causes? Certainly not. Maybe the team allowed an item that ended up being too big into the process. Maybe the team ignored an item once it had been pulled. Likewise, will there be external issues hiding in the shorter Cycle Times? Almost certainly. But at least I have shown you how to use a Scatterplot with percentile lines to begin the conversations about how to address those issues. Further, the more you adhere to the assumptions of Little's Law, the more confident we can be that the "up the stack" dots are due to outliers, and the "down the stack" dots are due to team policies.

Lastly, I have tried very hard not to use the language of the theory of variation (e.g., "special cause" and "common cause") as well as I have tried very hard not to use the language of Statistical Process Control (SPC). Not that I have anything against those approaches. Quite the opposite, in fact. I hold in very high regard the work of Shewhart and Deming. However, for most people and most purposes, going down an SPC path leads to academic debates about how to distinguish common cause from special cause, such as arguing over what specific statistical technique you should use for determining the upper and lower control limits (as discussed previously). These types of debates only serve to cause confusion and miss the point of what we are trying to accomplish anyway. Use the Scatterplot as a powerful way to visualize variation. But do not think it will magically categorize that variation for you. You are still going to have to inspect the dots, shapes, and patterns that emerge on your diagram. In other words, you are still going to have to think for yourself in order to get more predictable.

Conclusion

As with CFDs, the real purpose for analyzing a Cycle Time Scatterplot is to learn. To learn you should ask some familiar questions. "What's going on with our Cycle Time?" "Is what's going on a good thing or bad thing?" "If good, how can we keep doing it?" "If bad, what interventions could make things better?" A Scatterplot not only gets you to asking the right questions sooner, but will also suggest the right actions to take for increased predictability.

There are many things that contribute to the random scattering of dots present on most Scatterplots. You may have been surprised to find out that most of the causes of randomness are things we do to ourselves (well, maybe not so surprised had you been reading closely until now).

Now that we have a decent understanding of what Scatterplots are and how to interpret them, it is time to move on to how we might use our newfound knowledge to enhance our predictability via the Service Level Agreement.

Key Learnings and Takeaways

- The policies that you have in place will greatly influence the patterns and trends of dots that appear on your Scatterplot.
- Some qualitative things to look for on Cycle Time Scatterplots:
    - A triangle pattern that never flattens out
    - Clusters of dots (either high or low)

- Long periods of gaps in the data
- Extreme outliers
- Dots that just cross a give percentile line

Chapter 12 - Service Level Agreements

In Chapter 10 I explained how to use percentile lines as an aid to analyzing Scatterplot data. But what exactly are the percentile lines telling us?

To answer this question, we must first revisit some principles from the previous section. Recall that in one of the chapters on the Conservation of Flow (Chapter 8) I talked about the principle of just-in-time commitment. Just-in-time commitment helps us to balance the demand on the system with the system's capacity. However, there is a direct consequence of implementing this methodology. The other dimension of deferred commitment that does not really get talked about all that much is the necessity that we must—at the time of commitment—also communicate to our customers a date range and confidence level for each and every committed-to work item. For example, when we pull an item into our process we might tell our customers that we expect that item to flow all the way through to completion in fourteen days or less with 85% confidence level.

These date ranges and confidence levels are normally published as part of process visualization and are commonly known as "Service Level Agreements" or SLAs. Now, I personally hate the term SLA (I think Deming would too). SLA sounds too much like the language of formally negotiated contracts with penalties for nonconformance. That is really not what we are talking about here. What we are talking about is a reasonable expectation of service that a team is committing to for a particular item. A team or an individual should not be punished for missing these commitments (recall that I talked earlier about the term commitment with a small "c"). Rather, the team should take any missed SLA as an opportunity to learn. Why did we miss the SLA? Is there anything we can to do prevent that happening in the future?

Better nomenclature for the concept of a SLA, in my opinion, is "Service Level Expectation" or "Cycle Time Target". However, as SLA is the term most commonly used in our industry then I am going to adopt that vocabulary myself for our purposes in this chapter.

The way we determine what date range and confidence level that we can reasonably commit to is by looking at the percentile lines on our Scatterplot.

To explain, I want to refer you back to Figure 10.5. You can see in this diagram that the 50th percentile for the Cycle Times is 20 days, the 85th percentile is 43 days, and the 95th percentile is 63 days. That means that any item that enters our process has a 50% chance of finishing in 20 days or less, an 85% chance of finishing in 43 days or less, or a 95% chance of finishing in 63 days or less. Armed with this information we can sit down with our customers and ask them what kind of confidence level they would be most comfortable with. If they are ok with us missing our commitments 50% of the time, then the team would choose 20 days at 50% as its SLA. If, however, they want a greater confidence in terms of the team meeting its commitments, then the team may choose to go with an SLA of 43 days at 85%. To reiterate, the choice of a team's SLA should be made in close collaboration with their customers.

While there is no hard and fast rule on this, it is been my experience that most teams start out at the 85th percentile as their SLA. The goal of the team then should be to first meet that SLA at least 85% of the time (true predictability) but then also to bring down the total number of days that the 85th percentile represents over time. Part of process improvement is going to be to shift all the percentile lines down as much as possible (but no further!). A wider spread in those lines means not only a higher number of days that we must communicate for our SLA, but it also means that our process is suffering from more variability. Both of those things decrease our overall predictability.

Take the following example of Figure 12.1:

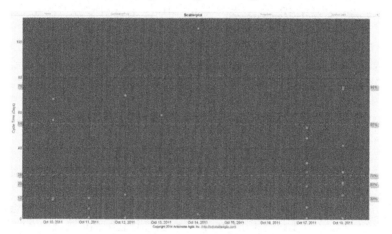

Figure 12.1: A Wider Spread in Percentiles

In Figure 8.6 the 50th percentile for the chart is 20 days, the 70th percentile is 25 days, the 85th percentile is 54 days, and the 95th percentile is 75 days. Think for a second about what an interesting conversation this would be when we present this data to our customers. At a 70% confidence, the team would require a 25 day or less SLA. But to go to an 85% confidence—that is just a 15% increase in confidence—the team would have to *more than double* their SLA from 25 days to 54 days!

This particular example is taken from a real world client of mine and, in this instance, the customer chose the 70% SLA to start out. Interestingly enough, though, the team, by implementing the strategies outlined in this book, was able to shift all of those percentile lines down over the course of the project such that by the end, the 85% percentile was now 25 days—exactly what the 70% percentile had been just months before. The team removed unnecessary variability, and, by definition, became more predictable.

I have just explained how to use standard percentiles to establish an SLA, but you might question, "How do I know if these standard percentiles are the right ones to use for my context?" Great question. The answer is that if you are just starting out, then those standard percentiles are most likely good enough. How you might detect if you need to move to another percentile more suitable for your specific situation is a more advanced topic that will need to wait for my next book. The point is that there is no hard and fast rule in terms of what percentile numbers to use. All I can say is begin with these standard ones and experiment from there.

Another question you might ask is, "How many data points do I need before I can establish an SLA?" The answer to that is—as always—dependent on your specific context. But I can tell you it is probably less than you think. As few as maybe 11 or 12. Probably no more than 30. The bigger question is in terms of quality not quantity. Instead of considering the number of dots, one question you may ask yourself is how well is your process obeying the assumptions of Little's Law in the producing those Cycle Times? The better you are at adhering to those assumptions, the fewer data points you will need. If you consistently violate some or all of the assumptions, then almost no amount of data is going to provide you a confidence level that you can be comfortable with.

The last thing I want to say about SLAs is that there are generally three mistakes I see when they are set. Those mistakes are:

1. To set an SLA independent of analyzing your Cycle Time data.
2. To allow an SLA to be set by an external manager or external management group.
3. Set an SLA without collaborating with customers and/or other stakeholders.

For the first point I want to say that there is nothing (necessarily) wrong with choosing an SLA that is not supported by the data. For example, let's say your data communicates that 85th percentile is 45 days. It would technically be ok to publish an SLA of 35 days at 85%. But at least make that decision in context after having reviewed what your Scatterplot is telling you.

The second mistake should be obvious, but it is worth reiterating. The whole point of an SLA is not to beat a team into submission or to punish them when they miss their commitments. Since it is the team who is making the commitment, it should be the team that chooses what that commitment point is. The only other party that should be involved in the decision to set an SLA should be a customer and/or other stakeholder.

Which brings me to the last point. We are nothing without our customers. As stated in Chapter 1, they are the whole reason for our existence. It is our professional obligation to design a process that works for them. Therefore, our customers should have a seat at the table when discussing what commitment confidence level is acceptable. They may surprise you. They may opt for a shorter Cycle Time SLA with a higher uncertainty. They may be fine with a longer Cycle Time SLA if that means greater certainty. Our customers and stakeholders almost certainly have contextual information that we do not that will have some bearing on our choice of an SLA. Listen to them.

SLAs for Different Work Item Types

In the chapter on Cumulative Flow Diagrams (Chapter 4), I talked about the strategy of filtering on different work item types to generate different views of your data. The same approach is available for us to use on Cycle Time Scatterplots. Let's say we had a dataset that included the work item types of user stories, defects, and maintenance requests. With this data we could generate a Scatterplot and corresponding percentile lines for the data that included all three work items. Or we could generate a Scatterplot that included data for just the user stories. Or one that included just the defects, or one for just the maintenance requests, or for some combination thereof. As with CFDs, any one of these data segmentations—and their corresponding analysis—is perfectly valid.

But why might we want to segment our data in this way? There are at least two answers to this question. The first might be that you have tagged the items that did not finish "normally" (e.g., were abandoned) and want to filter your data to show only those. Displaying only the abandoned items would give you a good visualization as to the time wasted on those activities. That might give rise to questions and conversations about how to minimize those occurrences.

The second reason for segmenting is that the Cycle

Time percentiles for a Scatterplot consisting of data for only the work item type of "story" are probably going to be much different from the Cycle Time percentiles for a Scatterplot consisting of data for only the work item type of "defect". Segmenting our data this way would allow us—if we wanted—to offer different SLAs for different work item types. For example, our SLA for user stories might be 14 days at 85% but for defects it might be five days at 85%.

I am reluctant to discuss this SLA segmentation now, because you have to be very careful here. Remember that all the assumptions of Little's Law still apply. If you are going to offer different SLAs for different work items types, then you have to you have to ensure that all the assumptions for Little's Law for each and every subtype are adhered to.

Offering different SLAs for different work item types is a fairly advanced behavior. If you are just starting out with flow principles, I would highly recommend just setting one global SLA for all your work items types and get predictable that way first. Ignore "conventional wisdom" that you have to design in things like Classes of Service up front and offer different SLAs for those different Classes of Service immediately. To put it delicately, I believe this type of advice is misguided (a fuller treatment of Class of Service and its dangers is presented in Chapter 13). If you are new to these metrics, begin by applying the principles presented in this book and then measure and observe. Get predictable at an overall system level first. You may find that is good enough. Only optimize for subtypes later if you really need to.

Right-Sizing

One last thing about percentiles and SLAs. Remember that in Chapter 8 I talked about the concept of just-in-time commitment and about how operating a pull system allows us to defer commitment to the last responsible moment. In that chapter I also talked about the consequence of deferring commitment is that we need to do what we can to make sure that—once committed to—an item has the best possible chance of flowing through the system to completing. One of those things we need to do is to perform a "right size" check on the item.

Before you ask, right-sizing does not mean you do a lot of upfront estimation and planning. Remember, this book emphasizes measurement and observation over estimation and planning. The SLA we have chosen is the measurement we are looking for. In other words, the SLA will act as the litmus test for whether an item is of the right size to flow through the system. For example, let's say we have chosen an SLA of fourteen days at 85%. Before a team pulls an item into the process, a quick question should be asked if the team believes that this particular item can be finished in fourteen days or less. The length of this conversation should be measured in seconds. Seriously, seconds. Remember, at this point we do not care if we think this item is going to take exactly five days or nine days or 8.247 days. We are not interested in that type of precision as it is impossible to attain that upfront. We also do not care what this particular relative complexity is compared to the other items. The only thing we do care about is we think we can get it done in 14 days or less. If the answer to that question is yes, then the conversation is over and the item is pulled. If the answer is no, then maybe the team goes off and thinks about how to break it up, or change the fidelity, or spike it to get more information.

Some of you out there may be arguing that right-sizing is a form of estimation. I would say that you are probably right. I never said that all estimation goes away. All I said was that the amount and frequency with which you do estimation will change. Think about all the time you have wasted in your life doing estimation. Think about all the time wasting in "pointless" debates of whether a story is two points or three points. Using these percentiles is a means to get rid of all of that. Measuring to get an SLA allows us to adopt a much lighter approach to estimation and planning. To me, this is one of the biggest reasons to gather the data in the first place.

Percentiles as Intervention Triggers

There is still another reason to look at our Cycle Time data percentiles as they pertain to SLAs. And to understand this other reason, we need to first talk about life expectancy.

According to a life expectancy calculator at WorldLife-Expectancy.com (at the time of this writing), a female born in the United States has a life expectancy of 85.8 years at the time of her birth. If she lives to be 5 years old, her life expectancy goes up to 86.1 years. If she lives to be 50, her life expectancy becomes 87.3 years. And if she lives to be 85 (her life expectancy at the time of her birth), her new life expectancy jumps to 93! This data is summarized in the following table:

Age	Life Expectancy at that Age (in Years)
Birth	85.8
5	86.1
50	87.3
85	93

Figure 12.2: Life Expectancies at Different Ages

It is a little known fact that the older you get, the longer your life expectancy is. That is due to the fact that the older you get the more things you have survived that should have killed you.

The exact same phenomenon happens with Cycle Time. Generally speaking, the older a work item gets, the greater chance it has of aging still more. That is bad. Remember, delay is the enemy of flow!

This is why it is so important to study the aging of work items in progress. As items age (as items remain in process without completing), we gain information about them. We need to use this information to our advantage because, as I have said many times before, the true definition of Agile is the ability to respond quickly to new information. To paraphrase Don Reinertsen, this new information should cause our tactics to change. The percentiles on our Scatterplot work as perfect checkpoints to examine our newfound information. We will use these checkpoints to be as proactive as possible to insure that work gets completed in a timely and predictable manner.

How does this work? Let's talk about the 50th percentile first. And let's assume for this discussion that our team is using an 85th percentile SLA. Once an item remains in progress to a point such that its age is the same as the Cycle Time of the 50th percentile line, we can say a couple of things. First, we can say that, by definition, this item is now larger than half the work items we have seen before. That might give us reason to pause. What have we found out about this item that might require us to take action on it? Do we need to swarm on it? Do we need to break it up? Do we need to escalate the removal of a blocker? The urgency of these questions is due to the second thing we can say when an item's age reaches the 50th percentile. When we first pulled the work item into our process it had a 15% chance of violating its SLA (that is the very definition of using the 85th percentile as an SLA). Now that the item has hit the 50th percentile, the chance of it violating its SLA has doubled from 15% to 30%. Remember, the older an item gets the larger the probably that it will get older. Even if that does not cause concern, it should at least cause conversation. This is what actionable predictability is all about.

When an item has aged to the 70th percentile line, we know it is bigger than more than two-thirds of the other items we have seen before. And now its chance of missing its SLA has jumped to 50%. Flip a coin. The conversations we were having earlier (i.e., when the item hit the 50th percentile line) should now become all the more urgent.

And they should continue to be urgent as that work item's age gets closer and closer to the 85th percentile. The last thing we want is for that item to violate its SLA—even though we know it is going to happen 15% of the time. We want to make sure that we have done everything we can to prevent a violation occurring. The reason for this is just because an item has breached its SLA does not mean that we all of a sudden take our foot off the gas. We still need to finish that work. Some customer somewhere is waiting for their value to be delivered.

However, once we breach our SLA we are squarely

in unpredictable land because now we cannot communicate to our customers when this particular item will
complete. For example, take a look at the figure below
(Figure 12.3):

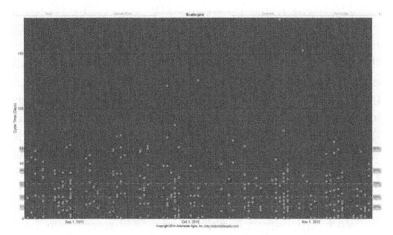

Figure 12.3: The Danger of Breaching an SLA

You can see in this chart that the 85th percentile is 43
days. But there is an item in late October that took 181
days to finish (do you see that isolated dot right at the
top of the chart?). That no man's land between 43 days
and 181 days (and potentially beyond) is a scary place to
be in. We want to do whatever we can not to have items
fall in there.

Conclusion

SLAs are one of the most important and yet least talked
about topics in all of Lean-Agile. SLAs not only allow
teams to make commitments at the individual work item
level, but they also give us extremely useful information about when teams need to intervene to ensure the
timely completion of those items. Further, if a team

follows all of the principles presented in this book, then the SLA can be used as a substitute for many upfront planning and estimation activities.

I began Chapter 11 by discussing how most of the reasons why we are not predictable is due to things under our control that we do to ourselves. One of the most common things we do to ourselves that hinders our predictability is not pay attention to the order in which items are pulled through our process. This problem is so common that I will devote the entirety of the next chapter to discussing its perils.

Key Learnings and Takeaways

- Use your Scatterplot's percentiles to collaborate with your customers in choosing a Service Level Agreement for your process (other terms for Service Level Agreement could be Service Level Expectation or Cycle Time Target).
- As with CFDs, it is possible to segment your data by type. You might choose to do this to offer different SLAs for different work item types in your process.
- SLAs allow for commitment (and estimation) at the work item level.
- SLAs provide a sense of urgency to items that have been committed to.
- You can also use Cycle Time data percentiles as a guide for "right-sizing" items that come into your process. Use this right-sizing as a shortcut for estimation.
- Comparing an item's age to its SLA can provide useful information about when to make an intervention to ensure timely completion.

PART FOUR - PUTTING IT ALL TOGETHER FOR PREDICTABILITY

Chapter 13 - Pull Policies

Most airports around the world allow access to the flight departure area if a person can prove that he is a passenger who is indeed flying that day. This proof usually takes the form of a valid boarding pass and a valid government-issued ID.

The United States is no exception to this rule. In the U.S., the Transportation Security Administration (TSA) is responsible performing passenger checks. TSA agents are stationed right before security and passengers wishing to get to the departures area must first check-in with these agents.

Many small airports in the U.S. staff only one TSA agent to perform traveler validation. At those small airports during busy periods, quite a long queue will form in front of the sole agent. Little's Law tells us that as more and more people join the queue, those people can expect to wait for longer and longer amounts of time to get through the checkpoint (on average). In this scenario, if you are a regular passenger, do you see the problem with predictability?

It gets worse.

In an attempt to streamline the process for what are considered low-risk passengers, the TSA has introduced something called "TSA Pre-check" (TSA Pre). Passengers who are certified as TSA Pre do not have to go through the whole security rigmarole of taking off shoes, taking off belts, taking off jackets, and removing laptops. That is great if you are TSA Pre. The problem is that you still have to go through the upfront TSA passenger validation outlined previously. However, the TSA has attempted to solve this problem by establishing a different lane for TSA Pre passengers to queue in to get their credentials checked. So now there are two lanes for two different types of passenger: a first lane called TSA Pre (as I have just mentioned) and a second lane that I am going to call "punter". In the small airports, unfortunately, there is still usually only one upfront, credential-checking agent to serve both of these lines. The TSA's policy is that whenever there is a person standing in the TSA Pre line, that the agent should stop pulling from the punter queue and pull from the TSA Pre queue. See a problem with overall predictability yet?

It gets worse.

In addition to a separate TSA Pre lane there is usually a separate "priority lane" for passengers who have qualified for elite status on an airline. These passengers still have to go through the same security checks as the other punters, but they do not have to wait in a long line to get the upfront ID check. To be clear, this is technically not a TSA thing, it is usually an airport/airline thing. However, at those small airports, it is the single TSA agent's usual policy to look at the TSA Pre line first. If there is no one there, she will look at the priority lane next and pull people from there. Only if there is no one in the TSA Pre or priority queue will the agent start to pull again from the punter line. See a problem yet?

It gets worse.

As I just mentioned, everyone who wants to get air side at an airport must go through this upfront ID check. Everyone. This includes any and all airline staff: pilots, flight attendants, etc. Crew members can usually choose whatever line they want to get their credentials checked (TSA Pre, Priority, or punter). Further, once they are in those lines, the crew are allowed to go straight to the front of their chosen queue regardless of how many people are ahead of them. At those small airports, the sole TSA agent first looks to see if there are any airline crew in line. If none, then they look to see if there are any TSA Pre passengers. If none, then they look to see if there are any priority passengers. If none, then they finally pull from the punter line. See a problem yet?

If you are in the punter line, guess what you are doing while that lone TSA agent pulls passengers from those higher priority queues? You got it: waiting. What do you think this is doing to the predictability of the punter queue? In other words, how many assumptions of Little's Law have been violated in this airport scenario? Is Little's Law even applicable here?

Class of Service

This airport screening example is a classic implementation of a concept known as Class of Service (CoS):

A Class of Service is a policy or set of policies around the order in which work items are pulled through a given process once those items are committed to (i.e., once those items are counted as Work In Progress).

That is to say, when a resource in a process frees up, CoS are the policies around how that resource determines what in-progress item to work on next. There are three subtleties to this definition that need to be addressed up front.

First, a Class of Service is different than a work item type (I spoke about how to segment WIP into different types in Chapter 2). This point can be very confusing because many a Kanban "expert" uses these two terms interchangeably. They are not. At least, not necessarily.

We can choose to segment our work items into any number of types and there is no prescription as to what categories we use for those types. Some previous examples I have given for work item types are user stories, defects, small enhancements, and the like. You could also segment work items into types using the source or destination of the work. For example, we could call a unit of work a finance work item type, or we could say it is an external website work item type. Or we could call a unit of work a regulatory work item type or a technical debt work item type. The possibilities are endless. And, yes, one of the ways you could choose to segment types is by Class of Service—but you do not have to. I have always thought a better way to apply CoS is to make it a dimension of an existing type. For example, a work item of type user story has an expedited CoS, a work item of type regulatory requirement has a fixed date CoS. But that is just personal preference. Just know that work item types and CoS are different. Do not let the existing literature out there on this stuff confuse you.

To be clear, you can have any number of types of Class of Service as well. The most talked about ones happen to be Expedite, Fixed Date, Standard, and Intangible. But those are only four examples of limitless kinds of Class of Service. Any time that you put a policy in place (explicit or not!) around the order in which you pull something through a process, then you have introduced a Class of Service.

The second subtlety of the above definition is that CoS does not attach until a work item has been pulled into the process. I cannot stress this point enough. There is absolutely no point in having a discussion about whether work item A is an Expedite (for example) and whether work item B is a Fixed Date while both items A and B are still in the backlog. The reason for this is, as I have mentioned so many times before, is that while those items are still in the backlog there is no confidence that either will ever be worked on. Additionally, it is entirely possible that once committed to, our SLA would predict that we need not give any preferential pull order to that item. For example, let's assume that it is February 1 when we pull a new item into our process. Let's further say that this new item has a due date of February 28, and that the SLA for our process is 11 days. In this case, our SLA would predict that this item will complete well before its due date so there would be no point in giving it any preferential treatment. Given both of these scenarios, why waste time determining the order of pull before an item is in the system? That is why the decision of what CoS to use happens only at the time of an item's first pull transaction.

Which brings me to the last subtlety about CoS. The order in which items are pulled once committed to is very different from the decision criteria around what item to work on next at input queue replenishment time. Again, this is a very subtle but very important distinction. The criteria for what items we pull next off the backlog are very different from the criteria around the order in which we pull those items once in progress. If this concept is still ambiguous to you, then hopefully I will have cleared it up by the end of this discussion.

The Impact of Class of Service on Predictability

In the last chapter, I mentioned that most teams do not understand how the improper implementation of pull policy—whether explicit or not—negatively impacts their system's predictability. They do not understand these negative impacts because CoS has either never been properly or fully explained to them. I would like to quantify these negative impacts by examining a pull policy scenario that I have set up for you.

In this particular example, we are going to be operating a process that looks like Figure 13.1:

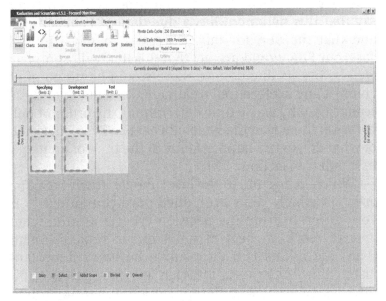

Figure 13.1: The WIP Limited Process in our Simulation

You will notice on this board that the Specifying column has a Work In Progress limit of two, the Development column has a Work In Progress limit of two, and the Test column has a Work In Progress limit of one. Let's further suppose that for this process we will be working through a backlog of 50 items. In this experiment, we are going to size all of our items such that each one takes exactly 10 days to go through each column. That is, every item in the backlog that flows through this board will take exactly 10 days in Specifying, 10 days in

Development and 10 days in Test. We are also going to introduce two Classes of Service: Standard and Expedite. I will explain the pull order rules for each of these as we go through the simulation. Lastly, you should know that in this experiment there will be no blocking events or added scope. We will start the simulation with 50 items in the backlog and we will finish the simulation with 50 items in Done. All items will be allowed to flow through unmolested.

Or will they?

You will notice from the design of the board in Figure 13.1 that, at the end of the 20th day, two items will have completed in the Dev column but there will only be space to pull one of those items into the Test column. As you are about to see, the simple decision around which of those two to pull will have a dramatic effect on the predictability of your system.

For the first run we are going to assign only a Standard CoS for work items on the board. Further, we are going to define a strict "First-In, First-Out" (FIFO) pull order policy for those Standard class items. That is, the decision around what item should be pulled next will be based solely on which item entered the board first.

Before I show you the results, I would like you to try to guess what the expected Cycle Time for our items will be. (Note: for these simulations I am going to consider the "expected value" for the Cycle Times to be the 85th percentile.) If you are ready with your guess then read on.

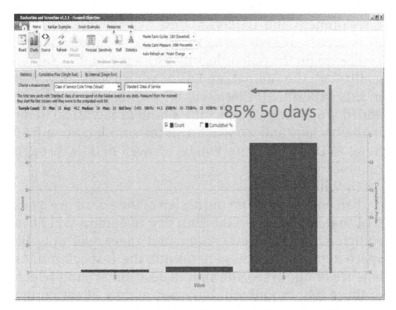

Figure 13.2: Strict FIFO Pull Order with No Expedites

Figure 13.2 shows a Histogram of the Cycle Time results. You can see that after running this simulation, the 85th percentile for our Cycle Times is 50 days. In other words, 85% of our items finished in 50 days or less. Also, as you look at the distribution of Cycle Times in the Histogram above, you will see that we have a fairly predictable system—there is not much variability going on here. But let's see what happens when we begin to tweak some things.

In this next round, we are going to replace our strict FIFO pull order policy with a policy that says that we will choose which item to pull next completely at random. One way it may help you to think about this is when two items are finished in the Development column, we are essentially going to flip a coin to see which one we should pull next into the Test column.

Any guess now as to what this new policy is going

to do to our expected Cycle Time? To variability? To predictability?

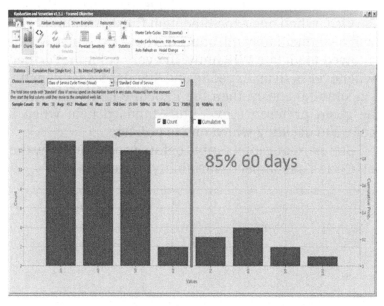

Figure 13.3: Random Pull Order with no Expedites

In this case (Figure 13.3), the simple switch from FIFO queuing to random queuing has increased our 85th percentile Cycle Time from 50 days to 60 days—that is an increase of 20%! Did you expect that such a minor policy change would have such a big Cycle Time impact? You can also see that the corresponding distribution (shown in Figure 13.3) is much more spread out reflecting the increased variability of our random decision making.

Things get interesting when we start to add in some expedites. Let's look at that next.

We are now going to go back to the pull policy where our Standard class items are going to be pulled through in a strict FIFO queuing order. The twist we are going introduce, though, is that we are now going to include an Expedite Class of Service for some of the items on our board. In this round we are going to choose exactly one item on the board at a time to have an Expedite Class of Service. When one expedited item finishes, another one will be immediately introduced. These Expedites will be allowed to violate WIP limits in every column. Further, whenever both an Expedite and Standard class item finish simultaneously, then the Expedite item will always be given preference over the Standard item when it comes to deciding which one to pull next.

Standard questions apply before proceeding: any thoughts on Cycle Time impact? Variability? Predictability?

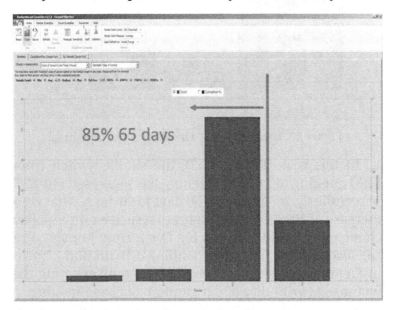

Figure 13.4: FIFO Pull Order with Always One Expedite on the Board

Any surprises here (Figure 13.4)? Compared to the previous case (the random pulling case), Expected Cycle Time has increased five days from 60 days to 65 days.

You can see the Histogram (Figure 13.4) has become much more compact, but there is still a wider spread than when compared to our baseline case (the strict FIFO/no expedites case), and, as I just mentioned, overall Cycle Times are longer. Did you expect this to be the worst case yet from a Cycle Time perspective? You can see that this is only marginally worse than the random queuing round—but it is still worse. That is an interesting point that bears a little more emphasis. In this context, introducing an Expedite CoS is worse for predictability than simply pulling items at random. Hopefully you are getting a feel for just how disruptive expedites can be (if you were not convinced already).

But we are not done yet. There is still one permutation left to consider.

In this final experiment, we are going to change our pull policies for Standard class items back to random from FIFO. We are going to keep the rule of always having one Expedite item on the board. The pull policies for the Expedites remain the same: they can violate WIP limits and will always get pulled in preference to Standard class items.

Now what do you think will happen?

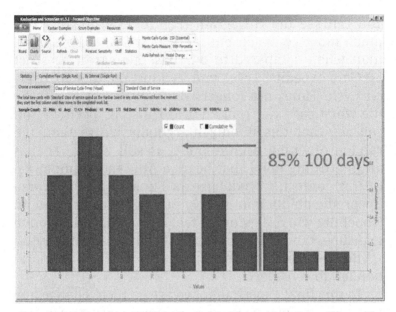

Figure 13.5: Random Pull Order with Always One Expedite on the Board

Expected Cycle Time in this scenario (Figure 13.5) has jumped to a simulation-worst 100 days! The spread of our data shown by the Histogram (Figure 13.5) is also worrying: Cycle Times range anywhere from 40 days to 170 days. If that is not variability, then I do not know what is. Remember, in the ideal system of the first case, the range of Cycle Times were 30 to 50 days.

Let's look at all these results side by side (Figure 13.6):

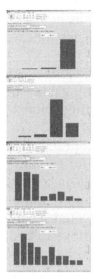 Strict FIFO (no expedites)

Strict FIFO always one expedite

Random Queuing (no expedites)

Random Queuing always one expedite

Figure 13.6: CoS Results Side by Side

I would like you to reflect on this result for a minute. Minor tweaks to process policies had a dramatic impact on simulation outcomes. Again, note that these policies were all things that were completely under our control! All of the variability in these scenarios was of our own doing. Worse still, my guess is that you have probably never even given any thought to some of these policies. Do you pay attention to how you decide what order to pull items through your process? Do you try to control or limit the number of Expedites on your board? Do you have any clue what a lack of these considerations is doing to your process predictability?

Obviously in the previous example I have controlled for story size. That is generally not possible (nor even required nor suggested) in the real world. Differences in story size are additional variability that is going to affect the predictability of the process and make these Histograms look even worse. That being the case, why

would we not try to mimic FIFO as closely as possible?
Why would we not try to control pull policies that we
can control?

The short answer is that we should. The longer answer is that in many contexts FIFO queuing may be
impractical (leaving the business value dimension of
pull decisions aside for a minute).

There are a couple of reasons for the impracticality
of FIFO queuing. Think about a restaurant, for example.
Patrons of restaurants do not flow through in a strict
FIFO ordering. To illustrate, let's say a group is seated
first at Table A. Then a different group is seated second
at Table B. The group at Table B does not have to wait
until the first group at Table A has finished before the
second group is allowed to leave. That would just be
silly. The groups are, however, usually seated in a First
In First Served (FIFS) order. A (mostly) FIFS scheme is
much more practical in the knowledge work context as
well and usually is the best strategy from a predictability
perspective.

Extending the restaurant example, let's say that a
group of four people arrives to an establishment that is
currently full and they need to wait for a table to open up
in order to be seated. Let's further say that a group of two
people arrives after the group of four and this second
group needs to wait as well. If the first table to open
up seats only two people, then it is reasonable that the
group of two—who arrived second—would be seated
first. This scenario happens all the time in knowledge
work. Maybe a resource frees up and is ready to pull
an item. But he does not have the expertise to work
on the item that has been waiting the longest (which
should be his first choice). From a practical perspective,
it would be reasonable for him to pull the item that has
been waiting the second longest (assuming, again, that

he has the right skills to work on that second one). But remember, even though this may be the best practical decision, it may not be the best predictable decision. In this scenario, what are some longer term improvements you could make for better predictability?

The point to all of this is that the further you stray from FIFO queuing, the less predictable you are. That is not to say that there are not practical reasons why you should forfeit FIFO. And by the way, arbitrary business value reasons and fictional Cost of Delay calculations do not fall into this practical category. But more on that a little later.

The most common objection I get when I explain why teams should adopt FIFO (or FIFS, or mostly FIFS) and dump expedites is that, "Expedites happen all the time in our context and we can't not work on them". They might go on to say that these expedites are unpredictable in size and number. Not only am I sympathetic to this argument, I acknowledge that this is the case for most teams at most companies.

Slack

So what is a team to do? Why, look at FedEx, of course.

Federal Express (FedEx) is an American shipping company that allows clients to send packages all over the world. For this example, though, let's limit the scope of our discussion to just the continental United States. Suffice it to say that FedEx knows a thing or two about flow and predictability, and the company is worth studying.

When a prospective customer wishes to ship a package via FedEx that customer has several service options to choose from. She can choose to it send overnight,

2nd day air, and standard ground—to just name a few. All of these service options are going to result in different CoS that FedEx uses in order to make sure that packages get to their destinations within the agreed SLA. Think about this for a second. In the U.S. there are thousands of locations that FedEx will need to pick up packages from. On any given day, it is impossible for FedEx to proactively and deterministically know the exact number of packages, their respective requested CoS, their full dimensions, weight, etc. that will show up at any one of their locations. They could have one shop that is swamped with overnight requests while another location remains relatively quiet. The magnitude of this problem is almost beyond comprehension.

The incredible thing is, while I have not used FedEx a lot, I can tell you that every time I have needed to send a package overnight it has arrived at its location on time. How does FedEx do it?

There are a lot of strategies that FedEx employs, but the one that is probably most important is that at any given time FedEx has empty planes in the air. Yes, I said empty planes. That way, if a location gets overwhelmed, or if packages get left behind because a regularly scheduled plane was full then an empty plane is redirected (just-in-time it should be said) to the problem spot. At any given time FedEx has "spares in the air"!

A lot of people will tell you that Lean is all about waste elimination. But imagine if the FedEx CFO was hyper-focused on waste elimination for process improvement. Would that CFO ever allow empty planes to be in the air at any given time for any reason? Of course not. Flying empty planes means paying pilots' salaries, it means burning jet fuel, it means additional maintenance and upkeep. Luckily for FedEx, they understand that Lean is not just about waste elimination, it is about the effective, efficient, and predictable delivery of customer value. FedEx understands all too well the variability introduced by offering different CoS. They know that, in the face of that variability, if they want to deliver on their SLAs they must have spares in the air. They have to build slack into the system. Pretty much the only way to predictably deliver in the face of variability introduced by different CoS is to build slack into the system. There is just no way around it.

So let's get back to the "we have expedites that we cannot predict and that we have to work on" argument. Armed with this information about variability and slack, what do you think would happen if you went to your management and said, "if we want to predictably deliver on all of the expedites in our process (to say nothing of all of our other work), we need to have some team members that sit around, do nothing, and wait for the expedites to occur." You better have your resume updated because after you get laughed out of the room you will be looking for a new job.

"Ok, so you cannot have idle developers," so-called CoS experts will tell you, "then what you need to do is put a strict limit on the number of expedites that can be in your process at any given time." They will further advise you that the limit on expedites needs to be as small as possible—potentially as low as a WIP limit of one. Problem solved.

Not at all.

This advice ignores two further fundamental problems of CoS. For the first I will need another example. In my regular Kanban trainings I am a big fan of using Russell Healy's getKanban board game. I like the game not because it shows people how to do Kanban properly, but because it does a great job of highlighting many of the errors in the advice given by so many Kanban experts.

One of those errors is the advised use of an expedite lane on a Kanban Board (or CoS in general). Now in this game, there is a lane dedicated for expedited items, and, further, there is an explicit WIP limit of one for that lane. This is the exact implementation of the strategy that I just explained. So what is the problem? At the end of the game, I take the teams through an analysis of the data that they generated while they played the simulation (using all the techniques that have been outlined in the previous chapters). The data usually shows them that their standard items flow through the system in about ten or eleven days at the 85th percentile. And the spread in the Cycle Time data of standard items is usually between three and 15 days. The data for the expedited items' Cycle Time show that those items always take three days or less. You can see that the policies those teams used to attack the expedites made them eminently predictable. You will also note that those policies also contributed to the variability in the standard items, but that is not what is important here. What is important here is what happens when we project this to the real world. Imagine now that you are a product owner and you see that your requested item is given a standard CoS. That means that the team will request eleven days to complete it. But if your requested item is given an expedited CoS, then that item gets done in three days. What do you think is going to happen in the real world? That is right: everything becomes an expedite! Good luck trying to keep to the WIP of the expedited lane limited to one.

But that is not the only problem. Let's say that you work at an enlightened company and that they do agree that there will only be one expedited item in progress at any given time. It turns out even that is not enough! In the simulation example above, we limited our expedited items to one but that still caused a sharp increase in Cycle Time variability. Why? Because there was always one expedited item in progress. If you are going to have an expedited lane, and you limit that lane's WIP to one, but there is always one item in it, then, I am sorry to say, you do not have an expedited process. You have a standard process that you are calling an expedited process, and you have a substandard process which is everything else.

 For all practical purposes, introducing CoS is one of the worst things you can do to predictability.

But, you might argue, the real reason to introduce CoS is to maximize business value (for the purposes of this conversation, I am going to lump cost of delay and managing risk in with optimizing for business value). I might be persuaded by this argument if I believed that it was possible to accurately predetermine business value. If you could do that, then you really do not need to be reading this book because your life is easy. Obviously, if you have a priori knowledge of business value then you would just pull items in a way that maximizes that value. However, most companies I work with have no clue about upfront business value. And it is not due to in-experience, incompetence, or lack of trying. The reason most companies do not know about an item's business value upfront is because that value—in most cases—is impossible to predict. As value is only determined by our customers, an item's true value can only be known once put in the hands of the customer. Sure, most companies will require a business case before a project is started and this business case acts a proxy for business value. But, as you know, most business cases are anywhere from pure works of fiction to out and out lies. Basing pull decisions on disingenuous arguments is suspect at best.

Let's put it another way. As I just mentioned, true business value can be determined only after delivery to the customer. Choices about what to work on and when, then, are really just you placing bets on what you think the customer will find valuable. By introducing CoS and by giving preference to some items in the process over other items means that you are gambling that the customer will find those preferred items more valuable. The problem is that when you lose that bet—and I guarantee you almost always will—you will have not only lost the bet on the expedited item, but you will have also lost the bet for every other item in progress that you skipped over.

Honestly, I am only mostly that cynical. I do believe that the business value of an item should be considered, but I believe it should only be considered at input queue replenishment time. After an item is placed in process then I believe the best long term strategy is to pull that item—and all other items—through the process as predictably as possible. After all, part of the business value equation is how long it will take to get an item done. If you cannot answer the question "how long?" then how much confidence can you really have in your business value calculation?

What about obvious high value expedites? Things like production being down that require all hands on deck? Or a new regulatory requirement that could result in massive fines for noncompliance? Obviously, those things will—and should—take precedence. But, just like the FedEx example, you should study the rate of occurrence for those items and adjust your process design accordingly. That will potentially mean lowering overall process WIP. That will probably mean making sure free resources look to help out with other items in process before pulling in new items. And so on.

To come full circle on our discussion about Little's Law that was started in Chapter 3, I hope it is obvious for you to see how CoS represents a clear violation of the fourth assumption of Little's Law (and potentially the first and the third as well). The central thesis of this book is that every violation of a Little's Law assumption represents a reduction in overall process predictability. CoS represents an institutionalized violation of those assumptions. How could you ever expect to be predictable when using CoS as your standard process policy?

Conclusion

It is obvious that to solve the problem outlined at the beginning of this chapter, the TSA could simply hire more agents. At the very least you would want to have a minimum of one agent per queue. This intervention would potentially solve the problem—or it would go a long way to alleviating it. Note that in this case, however, CoS would be eliminated. If each queue had its own server, then there would be no need for CoS. Wouldn't it be great if all our problems could be solved by just adding more people? The reality is that most companies do not have the money to keep hiring. That being the case, we want to make sure that we are using the resources we do have as efficiently as possible. That means choosing pull policies that maximize our resources' effectiveness and eliminating policies that make it harder for those resources to do their jobs predictably.

Although it probably sounds like it, I am not saying that CoS is inherently evil or that all CoS implementations are incorrect. I am, however, coming at this from the perspective of predictability. With that consideration, what I am saying is that you need to consider all aspects of CoS before implementing those policies. By definition, CoS will introduce variability and unpredictability into your process. The unpredictability manifests itself—among other things—as Flow Debt (Chapter 9). The truth is that the only part of your process that is more predictable with CoS is the highest priority class. Overall, CoS will cause your process to actually take a predictability hit (see Figures 13.4 and 13.5). Are you really that confident that the upfront value decisions that you are making with CoS are worth more than all the negative implications?

The arguments swirling around out there about why to use CoS are very seductive. The people making those arguments are very persuasive. I am hoping I have at least given you something to think about before assuming you should start with CoS as a default.

For me, the better strategy is to consider an item's forecasted value at queue replenishment time. Then, once in process, pull that item through while paying attention to all the concepts outlined in this and the previous chapters.

You have to know what you are doing before you do it. Build your process. Operate it using the policies for predictability that I have outlined thus far. Measure it. And then make a determination if CoS can help. Chances are you will never need CoS.

 Chances are you will never need Class of Service once you have a predictable process.

But what else do we need to consider ourselves predictable? I implied earlier that there are essentially to dimensions to being predictable:

1. Making sure your process behaves in a way it is expected to; and,
2. Making accurate predictions about the future.

Up until now we have mostly talked about point #1. It is time that we turn our attention to point #2.

Key Learnings and Takeaways

- Class of Service is the policy or set of policies around the order in which work items are pulled through a given process once those items are committed to (i.e., counted as Work In Progress).
- Class of Service only attaches at the point of commitment.
- Class of Service is different from queue replenishment.
- Assigning a work item a Class of Service is different from assigning a work item a type.
- Class of Service represents an institutionalized violation of some assumptions of Little's Law. This violation takes the form of Flow Debt which ultimately makes your process less predictable.
- The only way to predictably deliver using Class of Service is to build slack into the system.
- Instead of designing Class of Service into your process up front, consider other things you can do to eliminate or mitigate the need for them.
- Only introduce CoS after you have operated your process for a while and are confident that CoS is necessary. Still consider policies for CoS that mitigate their inevitable negative impact on flow.

Chapter 14 - Introduction to Forecasting

One of the definitions of predictability is the ability to make a quantitative forecast about a process's future state. Since forecasting is a part of predictability, I thought I would least say a few words about it.

A forecast is just a calculation about the occurrence of some future event. Yes, an estimate can be thought of as a forecast. But the forecasts that we are going to talk about in this chapter are going to be much more scientific than just some poor guy's best guess.

For the most part, we are going to be asked to make forecasts about the completion times for a given task, feature, project, etc., so for the purposes of this discussion let's limit ourselves to time forecasts. That means that from now on whenever I use the word "forecast" on its own, I am really referring to a "time forecast". Although, it should be said, that I believe the principles I am going to talk about here are applicable to any type of forecast.

Before we get any further, I would like to discuss is the necessary components of a forecast. You should never—and I mean never—communicate a forecast that does not include at least two things: a date range and a probability for that date range occurring.

 A forecast is a calculation about the future completion of an item or items that includes both a date range and a probability.

The future is full of uncertainty, and whenever uncertainty is involved then a probabilistic approach is necessitated (think quantum physics, the weather, etc.). A forecast without an associated probability is deterministic, and, as you know, the future is anything but deterministic.

With that said, let's get to some methods that you can—and, more importantly, cannot—use to develop a forecast. As this is an introduction, the methods outlined here are not meant to be all inclusive nor do I flatter myself to think that the treatment of the ones that I have chosen is exhaustive. For a richer discussion of these methods, please consult the references listed at the end of the book.

Little's Law

As I stated Chapter 3, using Little's Law to calculate a quantitative forecast is an incorrect application of the law. Little's Law is about examining what has happened in the past. It is not about making deterministic forecasts about the future. One of the reasons you cannot make deterministic forecasts with Little's Law is because it is impossible to predict which of the Law's assumptions will be violated in the future and how many times they will be violated. Remember, each violation of an assumption invalidates the exactness of the law.

Even if you could use Little's Law for projections, you would not want to. The reason is because it is a relationship of averages (arithmetic means). You never want to make a forecast based on an average. Average is a meaningless statistic unless you know something about the underlying distribution of the data from which the average was calculated. Specifically, when we are ignorant of the distribution, then we do not know what percentile we are talking about when we say the word "average". For example, depending on the shape of the distribution, the mean could be significantly less than 50%, exactly 50%, or significantly more than 50%.

But you will recall that with Little's Law we do not care about the probability distributions of the underlying stochastic processes. If we do not know the distribution, then we cannot give a probability of where the average falls. If we do not know a probability, then we cannot make a forecast. It is that simple.

Alternatively, using Little's Law for a gut check validation of a forecast for a *qualitative* determination is perfectly acceptable. But of course you would not want to make any staffing, cost, or project commitments based on these back-of-the-envelope calculation type calculations.

But what if we do know something about the underlying distribution? That knowledge could be extremely valuable. Further, I would argue it is worth investing in acquiring that knowledge. Any time we have distribution information we are going to run away from Little's Law for forecasting and toward some of the better techniques that follow.

Forecasts for a Single Item

What if you are asked to make a forecast about the completion of a specific work item, or epic or project? The answer to this question is actually very straightforward. In fact, I have already told you how to do it. In order to make a projection for a single work item, you will have to first collect the Cycle Time data for the all same types of work items à la the method I described in the Scatterplots chapter (Chapter 12). Once you have that data, it is a very simple exercise to answer the above question. You will just choose the percentile that you want to attach to your forecast and use the corresponding range. For example, look at the following Scatterplot for a team's user stories (Figure 14.1):

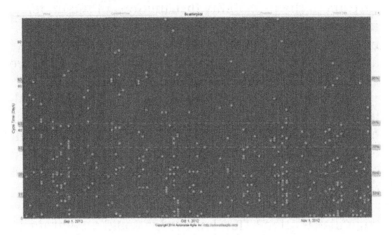

Figure 14.1: A Sample Scatterplot

A simple forecast that you could give using this data is that a typical work item completes in 43 days or less 85% of the time. And that is it. If the work items we are interested in were epics or projects, for example, then we would need to capture the Cycle Time data for epics or projects and then the approach to come up with a forecast for those work item types is exactly the same.

Straight Line Projections

I hate to belabor this point, but any CFD with a projection on it is not a CFD. It is a Burn Up chart or Projection Chart or something else, but it is most definitely not a CFD. To review, there are two reasons why a projections on CFDs are incorrect. The first reason is because to do a projection the chart must have some type of backlog displayed. But CFDs should not have backlogs on them. That is mistake number one. The second reason is that CFDs are for looking backward, they are not for making projections about the future. That is mistake number two. The fact that it is not a CFD is not a bad thing because this projection view can potentially be very useful (used incorrectly it can also be very bad). I should point out here that because I cannot call them CFDs, the term I am going to use for these types of charts is going to be either Burn Up Charts or Projection Charts.

Many teams are tempted to just perform a straight line projection off of the Throughput line on a Burn Up chart. The calculation—it is reasoned—is fairly simple. If a backlog has 100 items in it and the team is averaging 10 items per week, then it is easy to draw a trend line off the Throughput line and see where it intersects the backlog line as above. If you drop a line down to the X-axis at the point where the two lines intersect, then, voila, you have your release date.

There are so many problems with this approach that I am not sure where to begin. The first, and potentially most obvious since we just talked about it, is that once again this forecast is being based on an average. I have already discussed several reasons why you should not do that so I will not go into them here.

Secondly, over time, there is going to be variability in both the Backlog and Average Throughput. Depending on the time horizon under consideration, both the Backlog and Throughput can vary wildly (see the S-curve section below). Looking at this rather one-dimensional view of the world could cause managers to either panic or be overly confident depending on which way the variability pendulum swings on any given day.

Thirdly, there is no date range. That is one of our requirements for a proper forecast. No problem say the advocates. Let's draw an optimistic line for the backlog and a pessimistic line for the backlog. Likewise, let's draw an optimistic and pessimistic line for the Throughput trend line. Now we have several points of intersection for consideration that we can use for our completion date range. While I would agree that this is a much better view of the world, it still raises several questions. How were the optimistic and pessimistic backlog lines determined? The same should be asked of the Throughput lines. But most importantly, what is the probability of hitting this range?

A further complication of a straight line projection is that your completion rate over the long term is potentially not a straight line. As I mentioned before, any time you start a project with zero WIP and end with zero WIP, the resulting pattern of the Throughput line on the CFD mimics an "S-curve". Using a straight line to approximate an S-curve is problematic at best and dangerous at worst. There are overly complicated methods to approximate S-curves out there (again with no range and probabilities attached), and I am not going to get into them here, but I will say that the effort put into generating those forecasts would be better spent using more modern forecasting methods.

Just as with Little's Law, it is probably ok to perform a straight line projection for the purposes of a quick gut check on project status. But any insight you may gain is certainly not actionable. In fact, any action motivated by this strategy would probably be akin to tampering.

The thing is, however, if you put in place all the predictability measures that I have talked about in this book up until now, then straight line projections do not necessarily give results that are that bad. If you truly can keep continuous WIP, minimally violate the assumptions of Little's Law, not introduce CoS, then this type of approach might be good enough. If it is and it works for you, then, great, keep doing it. I am not going to tell you otherwise. But even so, we might be able to tweak things a little bit to give you more insight.

If you insist on using a Burn Up to do your projections, then might I suggest you augment your charts with the percentiles off of your Scatterplot? The way it would work is as follows. Start with your arrival and departure data for a CFD. Choose a completion date for your project (or release or whatever) and extend the timescale of the X-axis out to that completion date. Draw a vertical line up from the X-axis at that specific date. From your Scatterplot locate the Cycle Time for your 85th percentile (or whatever percentile you feel comfortable with). Take that 85th percentile Cycle Time and subtract it from your completion date. You can draw another line at this data and mark it "85th Percentile or something.

There are several advantages to this view. First, as with other projections of this nature, you know that any items that make up the Throughput line before the completion date are going to be in the release. Second, you know that any item that is started before that 85th percentile line has a greater than 85% chance of making the release. Any item started after that line has a less than 85% chance of making the release (you could draw subsequent percentile lines to communicate the diminished chance of late-started items of making the release).

Obviously, this chart will not tell you the exact number of items that will be in any given release (a better question to ask, by the way, is what is the likelihood of getting at least X number of work items finished by a particular date). But I would argue no chart out there will tell you that. Not deterministically anyway. As you approach the release date, you have a better and better understanding of the probability of items making it or not. Product owners (or customers) can then use that information to help guide them in the selection of what items should be started next. And that is probably about as good as you are going to get with a straight line projection approach.

Conclusion

In my experience, making a forecast for a single item's completion is very straightforward. Simply use the SLA method mentioned in Chapter 12.

Further, I do not recommend using Little's Law or a straight-line projection to make a forecast for a completion date. That is because both approaches are based on averages and neither give a probability of success.

If you really want to get good at probabilistic forecasting, then you are going to have to use a tool like the one we are going to talk about next: Monte Carlo Simulation.

Key Learnings and Takeaways

- A proper date forecast includes both a range and a probability.
- To forecast the completion of a single item use SLAs the method for calculating them outlined in Chapter 12.
- Do not use Little's Law for forecasting.
- Do not use averages for forecasting.
- Straight line projections are problematic because they are based on averages and because they do not communicate a probability of success.

Chapter 15 - Monte Carlo Method Introduction

In 1873, a Yorkshire cotton industry engineer named Joseph Jagger walked into a casino in Monte Carlo. Several days later he walked out of the casino with what amounted to close to over three million dollars (in today's money) having "broke the bank". In all truthfulness, though, during Jagger's run the casino itself never actually ran out of money (although the croupier's bank at the table did). But the story's place in popular culture had been cemented.

About seventy years later, a group of physicists working on nuclear fission problems at Los Alamos Laboratory in New Mexico named a method of using a statistical approach to solving complicated equations after a casino in Monte Carlo. Coincidence? Well, not really.

What did the two events have in common other than the name Monte Carlo? It was the recognition that a statistics could be used to solve highly complex problems.

At its simplest, the Monte Carlo Method (or Monte Carlo simulation) can be thought of as experiments with random numbers. The method is normally applied to highly uncertain problems where direct computation is difficult, impractical, or impossible. It has proved a useful tool in all kinds of fields like nuclear physics (which we just saw) oil and gas exploration, finance, insurance, etc. Given the uncertainty in knowledge work it seems strange that our industry has been rather late to the Monte Carlo game. One might argue that it has taken the emergence of modern agile methods to get us to the point where would could even model the work that we do for simulation. Regardless, I firmly believe that the Monte Carlo Method is the future of forecasting in knowledge work. Teams and companies that get this idea will survive. The others will not.

To offer a glimpse of how to perform a Monte Carlo Simulation, I offer this snippet from Wikipedia:

Monte Carlo methods vary, but tend to follow a particular pattern:

1. Define a domain of possible inputs.
2. Generate inputs randomly from a probability distribution over the domain.
3. Perform a deterministic computation on the inputs.
4. Aggregate the results.

The intricacies and practices about how to model and simulate knowledge work using the Monte Carlo Method are well beyond the scope of this book. Anyone truly interested in applying this method to knowledge work should review Troy Magennis' work on Lean Forecasting. I am not going to reproduce all of that information here. Rather, my goal is to discuss why flow principles and flow metrics are necessary to make a Monte Carlo approach more actionable. Operating your process in the manner that I have explained up until now is going to make it much easier for you to build more accurate models. More accurate models will lead to more accurate forecasts. And that is, after all, what we are all looking for.

As always, for the purpose of clarity, there are a couple of things I need to mention first. From this point forward I am going to use the terms "Monte Carlo Simulation" and "The Monte Carlo Method" interchangeably (my apologies to the purists out there). Further, I am going to categorize Monte Carlo Simulations into two cases: the case when you have data and the case when you do not. For the latter situation (when you do not have data), you are forced to choose a probability distribution for the value or values that you are trying to simulate. This choice quickly gets into a philosophical debate around what is the best type of probability distribution to use. As you may have guessed, I have never been one to shy away from a good debate; however, I believe this one is fairly academic. That is why, for the rest of this chapter, I am going to focus on the case when you do have data with which to simulate.

What Data to Use

This brings me to my first advice when doing Monte Carlo Simulation: if you have the data, use the data. If you do not have the data, then get the data (mine it or measure it), and use the data. Even if you are forced to pick a distribution when performing your first simulation because you have no data, you should quickly do what you can to gather real data to replace the original artificial distribution in your model.

I want to emphasize that by "gather real data" what I mean is to measure the basic metrics of flow from a process that utilizes all of the techniques outlined in this book. If you have an intrinsically unstable process, then that process might not be a great candidate for Monte Carlo Simulation. For example, one indication that your process data might not be suitable for Monte Carlo simulation is if you have a CFD that looks like Figure 7.5 (where arrivals far outpace your departures). In Chapter 7 I showed that Figure 7.5 demonstrates a scenario where Cycle Times are constantly increasing. Ever increasing Cycle Times mean that any selection of data from a past timeframe is a poor indication of what might happen in a future timeframe. This problem is mostly eliminated if you operate a process that looks like Figure 7.8 (where arrivals match departures).

However, getting to a process that produces a CFD like Figure 7.8 is not necessarily good enough. Another "smell" that our data might not be suitable for Monte Carlo Simulation is if we have a triangle-shaped Scatterplot as shown in Figure 11.1. A triangle pattern on a Scatterplot is also the result of an inherently unstable process. Recall that even if you have a CFD that looks like Figure 7.8, you still can have a Scatterplot that looks like Figure 11.1. The culprit in that scenario is Flow Debt. Large accumulations of Flow Debt destabilize a process and make it imminently unpredictable. Could you throw the Cycle Time data from Figure 11.1 into a Monte Carlo Simulation? Yes. Would the resulting forecast be reasonable? Probably not.

Your Model's Assumptions

The second thing you need to you need to know about Monte Carlo Simulations is that you need to be keenly aware of assumptions. I am not just talking about the assumptions built into your model, but I am also talking about the assumptions built into how whatever tool that you use (I am assuming you are using a tool for Monte Carlo Simulations) implements those assumptions. The accuracy of your model—and I cannot emphasize this enough—is going to depend on how well you match your process policies (that is, the day-to-day rules around how you operate your process) to all assumptions in the model and simulation tool.

 Your model's ability to produce an accurate forecast is going to depend on how well you match your process policies to your model's assumptions.

For example, let's revisit the scenario that I outlined in the Class of Service chapter (Chapter 13). In that simulation, we had a Kanban board that looked like Figure 15.1:

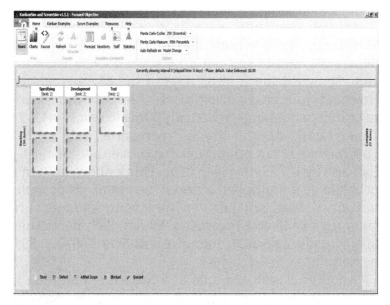

Figure 15.1: A Kanban Board Used as a Model for Monte Carlo Simulation

Now let's say that you have modeled the case where

you have Standard items and Expedite items and that you can only have one Expedite item on the board at a time. Further, let's say that Expedite items can violate WIP limits and can block other Standard items to complete. Let's assume you have modeled all of that correctly. But let's say that you did not model any policies around the order of pull between Standard items that finish at the same time.

Additionally, let's say that the tool you are using defaults to a strict FIFO pull order in the absence of any other policy being modeled. Finally, let's say that your actual day-to-day process uses (without explicitly stating it) a purely random pull order for Standard items. To be clear, in this scenario, we have a mismatch between the tool which assumes strict FIFO and your implicit process policy that assumes a random pull order.

Do you remember what is going to happen here? Your simulation—because it assumed FIFO for Standard items—is going to spit out a forecasted Cycle Time for your Standard items of 65 days at the 85th percentile. However, your real-world process—because you are using random queuing—is actually going to result in Cycle Times of 100 days at the 85th percentile. Due to that one missed assumption, you have over-optimistically forecast by up 35 days *per item*! Think about how this problem gets multiplied if you have hundreds of items in your backlog. What do you think your customers are going to say if you forecast a 65-day 85th percentile, but actually operated your process at a 100-day 85th percentile?

Another classic example of a missed assumption is when there is an open WIP spot but an item was not pulled immediately. Consider a scenario where you are operating a process that produces the following Kanban board:

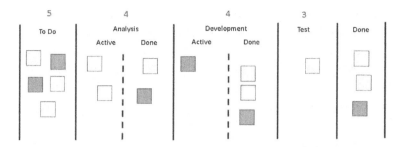

Figure 15.2: An Example Kanban Board

In Figure 15.2, you can see that the Test column has a WIP limit of three, but there is only one item in it. Further, you can see there are three items in the Development Done column that are waiting to be pulled. Let's also say that the board has been in this state for several days. However, the tool that you used to model this process never allows this condition to happen. That is to say that the Monte Carlo Simulation tool automatically and immediately pulls an item from Dev Done to Test whenever Test has space under its WIP Limit. Can you see that in your real world process that your items are aging longer than they were simulated to have done? That is a problem.

The moral of the story is that you have to use the assumptions in your model (both explicit or implicit) as actionable interventions to take while you are actually operating your process, or you have to take action to change the assumptions in the model to match the real world as it unfolds. When you get this right, then a Monte Carlo strategy is the going to be one of the most powerful predictive tools in your arsenal.

The thing to know about Monte Carlo simulation is that there is no one predicted outcome. Sampling a probability distribution will lead to thousands of possible outcomes that then, in turn, need to be analyzed in terms of the probability that they will indeed occur. Once you have obtained a forecast using Monte Carlo, your job is not done. It is not just set it and forget it. You need to actively manage to the assumptions in the model or change the model assumptions based on new information.

Conclusion

To be successful in forecasting, you have to first know what constitutes the proper form of a forecast and then you have to understand what methods are your friends in terms of developing reliable forecasts.

Even the best forecasting methods, however, are going to be only as good as the data they are based on. The first step in building a reliable forecast is to put in place a predictable process such that you can have confidence in the data that you are collecting. A forecast put together using bad data (from an unstable system, for example) produces something that either no one will like or no one will believe (this is the GIGO principle: Garbage In, Garbage Out). No forecasting method is going to be a suitable substitute for either (a) common sense thinking or (b) active management interventions as suggested by new information.

A forecast based on sound data that has been produced by a process that incorporates all the policies of predictability mentioned earlier is going to be defensible in the face of any challenge or criticism. At that point you have done your best. Let the chips fall where they may.

Key Learnings and Takeaways

- Monte Carlo Simulation is one of the best methods for coming up with a reasonable forecast.
- If you have data, then use that data to build your simulation models. If you do not have the data, then collect it and update your model(s)!
- Things to remember about Monte Carlo Simulation:
  - You must understand the assumptions of the model.
  - You must understand how your chosen simulation tool is implementing those assumptions.
  - Most importantly, you have to manage to those assumptions!

Chapter 16 - Getting Started

Hopefully I have convinced you by now that if you want your process to be predictable then you need to adopt the flow metrics and analytics that have been presented in this book. But how do you get started? I would not be doing my job if I did not give you at least some pointers on how to begin.

Defining Your Process

It may seem obvious or trivial to you, but the very first thing you need to do to get started is define the boundaries of your process. As I mentioned in Chapter 2, you must first decide on a point at which you consider work to have entered (or arrived to) your process. You must then decide the point at which you consider work to have exited (departed from) your process. Starting with a definition of your process boundaries is essential as any work items between these two boundaries can be considered WIP.

Remember that these boundaries are independent of any sprint or iteration definition. That is to say, if you use sprints or iterations to manage your process then it is possible for work to arrive at any time during the sprint and it is possible for work to depart at any time during the sprint. This concept may seem anathema to Scrum purists, yet the possibility remains. That means that any time work comes into your process—regardless of whether it is the beginning of a sprint or not—you need to count that work as arrived. Likewise, if any work exits your process—regardless of whether it is the end of a sprint or not—you need to count that work as departed.

The next thing you need to decide is which items that fall between those two boundaries will count as WIP. As I also mentioned in Chapter 2, the choice of items to call WIP is up to you, but make that choice and start tracking. As with anything, you can always tweak that decision later as you learn more.

Lastly, consider which of your existing policies are in direct violation of the assumptions of Little's Law. Do you not explicitly control arrivals by matching them to departures? Do you make sure that everything that starts eventually completes (or at least tag and track items that do not complete properly)? Do you let items arbitrarily age due to poor pull decisions (Class of Service, blockages, queuing, etc.)? If you currently operate your process in blatant violation of Little's Law, then you may want to think about changes to implement to get your process more aligned with that law. Remember that each violation of one of Little's Law's assumptions hampers your ability to be predictable.

Capturing Data

Once you have decided on your process policies, now all you have to do is capture the data. This is both easier and harder than it sounds. To answer why, we must consider two cases.

The first case we need to consider is if you are tracking data manually (i.e., independent of any other Agile tooling). In this case, you need to physically record the date that each work item enters each step of your workflow. For example, let's say your workflow is Analysis Active, Analysis Done, Development Active, Development Done, Test, Done. In this process, you would need to document the day that each item entered each state. An excerpt of what that data might look like is shown in Figure 16.1:

Story_ID	Analysis Active	Analysis Done	Development Active	Development Done	Testing	Done
1	06/25/2012	06/25/2012	06/26/2012	06/28/2012	06/29/2012	06/29/2012
2	06/25/2012	06/25/2012	06/27/2012	06/29/2012	06/29/2012	06/29/2012
3	06/21/2012	06/21/2012	06/21/2012	06/27/2012	06/27/2012	07/02/2012
4	06/21/2012	06/21/2012	06/21/2012	06/27/2012	06/27/2012	07/02/2012
5	06/21/2012	06/21/2012	06/21/2012	06/28/2012	07/02/2012	07/02/2012
6	06/21/2012	06/22/2012	06/22/2012	06/28/2012	06/28/2012	07/02/2012
7	06/25/2012	06/25/2012	06/25/2012	06/26/2012	06/29/2012	07/02/2012
8	06/25/2012	06/25/2012	06/25/2012	06/26/2012	06/29/2012	07/02/2012
9	06/21/2012	06/22/2012	06/22/2012	06/28/2012	06/28/2012	07/03/2012
10	06/25/2012	07/02/2012	07/02/2012	07/05/2012	07/06/2012	07/06/2012

Figure 16.1: Example Collected Data

You will remember that this approach was outlined in Chapter 4 (including how to handle the case when items move backward in your process), and I will refer you to that Chapter for a more detailed explanation.

You may want to further augment your data with certain item attributes. That is to say, you may want to capture which team worked on an item, what type it was (for example, user story, defect, etc.), if it finished normally—to name just a few examples. The attributes you choose to decorate your data are completely up to you. The reason you will want to do this, however, is those attributes will serve as filter points later. For example, maybe we only want to see data from Team A. Maybe we only want to see data for defects. Maybe we want to see all the items that got cancelled while in progress. Tagging data with appropriate attributes is a powerful practice that will enhance your understanding of overall process performance.

The second case you may need to consider is when you are using an electronic Agile tool to manage your work (e.g., VersionOne®, Jira, or the like). In this case we need to mine the data out of that tool so that it looks something like Figure 16.1. That is easier said than done. The problem is that most Agile tools do not track data in this way. That is not necessarily the fault of the tool—they were not designed with a flow metrics approach in mind. However, it does mean that it will require some work on your part to get your data in the format as shown in Figure 16.1. Luckily for us, most electronic tools offer an API (or direct access via SQL) to get to the data. The algorithm needed is going to be tool-specific and is beyond the scope of this book, so I will not going into any detail here. Keep in mind, though, that you are still going to have to handle the special cases of work flowing backward, work skipping steps, work being cancelled versus closed, etc. Also remember that you will want to mine the same item metadata that I just mentioned (type, team, etc.) to allow us to filter the data later.

Another word of caution that I need to mention about both cases is that your data is only as good as your use of your Agile tracking tool—whether that tool be an electronic system or a physical board.

 Your data is only as good as your use of your Agile tracking tool.

What I mean by that is no data extraction scheme will make up for abusing either your electronic or physical board. If work items are not updated in a timely manner, or blockers not captured properly, or items are moved back and forth randomly, then that lack of attention to process policies will be reflected in your data. You will then be forced to make the awkward decision to either try to fix the data or discard it altogether. It is a much better strategy to make sure all team members use your Agile tracking tool in an agreed upon matter so that you can have confidence in any subsequently collected data.

How Much Data?

"How much data do I need?" is one of the most common questions I get when introducing these methods to my clients. Most people assume you need copious amounts of data in order to glean any useful information. That is not necessarily correct. While more data is generally better, the truth is that less (often much less) data can be good enough.

For example, Douglas Hubbard (whose book "How to Measure Anything" is listed in the Bibliography) advises his clients on his "Rule of Five":

 Rule of Five – There is a 93.75% chance that the median of a population is between the smallest and largest values in any random sample of five from that population.

Recall from Chapter 10 that the median is the 50th percentile line on our Scatterplot. The Rule of Five seems remarkable but it is true (please see Hubbard's book for a detailed proof as to why this rule works). If you think of your process as a random Cycle Time number generator, then you will have a very good idea of where the median of your Cycle Time data is after only five items complete.

While powerful, the Rule of Five only gets us to the median of our population—which is actually not a bad place to start. But how much more data do we need to have confidence in the overall bounds of our process's Cycle Time? To answer that, let's consider a dataset that is uniformly distributed. A uniform distribution assumes that all samples from its population are equally probable. The textbook example of a uniform distribution is rolling a fair, six-sided die. All numbers on the die have an equal chance of coming up on each throw. If you were to plot the results of several rolls, what would emerge over time is a histogram with equal-height bars for each number on the die. Uniform distributions are interesting to study as they have several useful properties. For example, let's say we have eleven samples from a uniformly distributed population. The fact that we know we have a uniform distribution means that there is a 90% probability that the next sample (i.e., the 12th sample) will be between the min and the max of the previous eleven samples. That means that we have a fairly good understanding of the range of our uniform distribution after having collected only eleven data points. Our Cycle Times for our processes are not going to be uniformly distributed (please see Chapter 10a for more info), so we are going to need more than eleven samples to gain insight to our world, but not much more.

I mention the Rule of Five and Uniform Distributions to give you a feel for the greatly increased knowledge that can be gained after observing only a few data points. Do not think you need to collect hundreds or thousands of samples over several months to have any confidence in what your data is telling you. Probability is on your side here. Trust that you are getting very valuable feedback with even a very small data set.

Some Pitfalls to Consider

Once you have enough data in the correct format then it is just a matter of creating the associated flow analytics. Creating CFDs, Scatterplots, Histograms, etc. is fairly straightforward using a tool like Microsoft's Excel. All you need to do is turn the above dates into WIP counts for the CFD, and subtract the first date in the workflow from the last date in the workflow to calculate Cycle Time for the Scatterplot and Histogram. Again, I would strongly caution against using guidance found on many popular websites to do this because (a) those websites do not assume you have your data in the proper format, and (b) the instructions they give can lead to improperly constructed analytics.

While Excel may be a great tool to use when just starting out, you will no doubt quickly run into some limitations with that particular software package. First and foremost, Excel offers only a static view of your data. It does not allow you to readily interact with your analytics such as dynamically zooming in on a particular part of the graph, easily filtering out different types of work items, doing on the fly metrics calculations, and so forth. Secondly, Excel can become a bit unwieldy if managing thousands or tens of thousands of rows of data spread across multiple teams or departments. Still, Excel is not a bad option when starting out to make some quick progress.

You should also know that most major Agile tools vendors include some basic form of the analytics presented in this book. You might be asking yourself why you cannot just use the analytics included with your favorite tool. There are several answers to this question. And each answer must be considered carefully.

The first thing to consider is that while it is true that

most tools ship with something called a "Cumulative Flow Diagram" I have yet to see an electronic tool that generates a CFD correctly (barring the one that I will discuss shortly). The telltale sign that a CFD has not been constructed properly is if it has lines on it that go down. I explained why this is the case and introduced it as CFD Property #2 in Chapter 4, but it is worth reiterating here:

 CFD Property #2: Due to its cumulative nature, no line on a CFD can ever decrease (go down).

Any time you see a CFD that has one or more lines go down, then you can immediately tell that whoever constructed that CFD did not account for arrivals and/or departures correctly. Not accounting for arrivals and departures properly invalidates any resultant analysis of your chart.

To illustrate the point a little better, if you are currently using an electronic tool for reporting, have it generate its CFD for you. If you do not see any lines on the chart that go down, that is a good sign. However, as a test, try to "turn off" some of the latter workflow steps (if you can) starting from the bottom up. Do you see any of the remaining lines go down now? If so, it is a safe bet that the overall CFD has not been built according to all of the required CFD principles.

The second telltale sign that a CFD is suspect is if it contains a state called "Backlog". Strictly speaking, there is nothing wrong with displaying a backlog on a CFD, but the question remains how is the tool calculating the overall process approximate average Cycle Time (does it even call this calculation an approximate average Cycle Time or does it lead you to believe it is an exact

Cycle Time)? Again, I refer you to CFD Property #1 from Chapter 4:

 CFD Property #1: The top line of a Cumulative Flow Diagram *always* represents the cumulative arrivals to a process. The bottom line on a CFD *always* represents the cumulative departures from a process.

This property demands that overall process approximate average Cycle Time always be calculated from the top line of a CFD through to the bottom line of a CFD. If your chart includes a backlog and your tool's computed Cycle Time does not include the time spent in the backlog, then, again, you should be skeptical about whether the tool is calculating flow metrics properly.

Another pitfall to watch out for is how your Scatterplot is generated—assuming your tool even generates a Scatterplot. Your tool may call its Scatterplot a "Control Chart"—which it most certainly is not. As I mentioned in Chapter 10, why Control Charts (at least Control Charts in the Shewhart and Deming tradition) are probably not applicable to knowledge work is beyond the scope of this book. The thing you need to watch out for, though, is that if your tool takes a "Control Chart" approach, it is almost certainly assuming that your data is normally distributed. When looking at your Agile tool's Control Chart, look to see if displays lines that say something like "mean plus one standard deviation" or "$\mu + \sigma$". It might also give you an associated percentage akin to the standard percentages that I demonstrated in Chapter 10. In this case, that percentage is going to be based on an assumption that your data is normally distributed—which I can guarantee it is not. How do I know it is not? Look at your Histogram. You may remember from your statistics training that the shape of a normal distribution is a bell curve. When you look at your Histogram you will see that your data does not follow a bell curve pattern.

Using the mean plus a standard deviation (or the mean plus any number of standard deviations) approach and then associating the result with percentiles is dangerous given that your data is not normally distributed. You will get calculation errors that are not insignificant and you will potentially make poor decisions based on bad data.

The moral of this story is that when you are starting out with this type of analysis, do not necessarily trust the data or charts that your Agile tool displays for you. Do not trust its associated calculations. It may seem tedious, but I would encourage you to initially track some sample data yourself and then compare it to what your electronic tool generates for you. You may be surprised at how different those results can be. And when those results are different, which method will you trust more?

I hope you will forgive the shameless plug, but your other option is to use the ActionableAgile™ Analytics tool (available at https://actionableagile.com). That tool has been designed from the ground up with flow metrics and flow analytics in mind. You can be sure that if you get your data in the correct format (Figure 16.1) then putting that data into the ActionableAgile™ Analytics tool will result in flow analytics that are generated correctly. But, again, do not take our word for it. Collect the data yourself and validate any results independently.

Conclusion

I am going to wrap up this book (the next chapter) by taking a look at one of the largest and most successful implementations of using Actionable Agile Metrics for Predictability. The examples from the next chapter combined with an understanding of how to avoid the common pitfalls outlined here should have you well on your way to a predictable process.

But before you read the case study, let's take a minute to review what we have learned so far.

The steps to predictability are simple:

1. Set process policies based on the assumptions of Little's Law—including policies around how you define the boundaries of your process.
    a. Do not start new work at a faster rate than you finish old work.
    b. Do not allow items to age arbitrarily due to blockages, too much WIP or poor pull policies (Class of Service).
    c. Minimize the amount of work that is started but never finishes.
2. As you operate your process, collect data on the basic metrics of flow.
    a. Work In Progress
    b. Cycle Time
    c. Throughput
3. Visualize your flow metrics in flow analytics.
    a. Cumulative Flow Diagrams
    b. Cycle Time Scatterplots and Histograms
4. Use the analytics to take action.
    a. Intervene when your process goes awry
    b. Identify improvements to policies to improve performance

    c. Make forecasts

If you do these things, I promise that you will be predictable. You will be able to answer the question "When will it be done?"

Just as delay is the enemy of flow, any delay in implementing these principles severely hampers your ability to be predictable. Remember, the actions we take today have the biggest impact on our predictability tomorrow.

Good luck!

PART FIVE - A CASE STUDY FOR PREDICTABILITY

Chapter 17 - Actionable Agile Metrics at Siemens HS

In the interest of full disclosure, this case study has been previously published on two different occasions. One version appeared on the InfoQ website and the other on the Agile Alliance website. Bennet Vallet and I have also presented these results at conferences all over the world. I have included another slightly modified version here partly for your convenience, but mostly because it remains, at the time of this writing, the largest and most successful application of using actionable metrics for predictability. If you want some ideas on how to use the concepts of this book for your particular situation, this case study is a great place start.

Before you get started reading, however, you should know that this case study assumes that you are familiar with the concepts of the metrics of flow (Chapter 2) and their relationship via Little's Law (Chapter 3). Further, this case study assumes that you are familiar with how these metrics are visualized via Cumulative Flow Diagrams (Chapter 5) and Cycle Scatterplots (Chapter 10). Some familiarity with Kanban and its practices is also useful but not required.

This case study is written from the perspective of Bennet Vallet who partnered with me to write up his experience with Actionable Agile Metrics.

Introduction

Siemens Health Services (HS) provides sophisticated software for the Healthcare industry. HS had been using traditional Agile metrics (e.g., story points, velocity) for several years, but never realized the transparency and predictability that those metrics promised. By moving to the simpler, more actionable metrics of flow we were able to achieve a 42% reduction in Cycle Time and a very significant improvement in operational efficiency. Furthermore, adopting flow has led to real improvements in quality and collaboration, all of which have been sustained across multiple releases. This case study describes how moving to a continuous flow model augmented Siemens' agility and explains how predictability is a systemic behavior that one has to manage by understanding and acting in accordance with the assumptions of Little's law and the impacts of resource utilization.

History

Siemens Health Services, the health IT business unit of Siemens Healthcare, is a global provider of enterprise healthcare information technology solutions. Our customers are hospitals and large physician group practices. We also provide related services such as software installation, hosting, integration, and business process outsourcing.

The development organization for Siemens HS is known as Product Lifecycle Management (PLM) and consists of approximately 50 teams based primarily in Malvern, Pennsylvania, with sizable development resources located in India and Europe. In 2003 the company undertook a highly ambitious initiative to develop Soarian®, a brand new suite of healthcare enterprise solutions.

The healthcare domain is extremely complex, undergoing constant change, restructuring, and regulation. It should be of no surprise that given our domain, the quality of our products is of the highest priority; in fact, one might say that quality is mission critical. Furthermore, the solutions we build have to scale from small and medium sized community hospitals to the largest multi-facility healthcare systems in the world. We need to provide world class performance and adhere to FDA, ISO, Sarbanes–Oxley, patient safety, auditability, and reporting regulations.

Our key business challenge is to rapidly develop functionality to compete against mature systems already in the market. Our systems provide new capabilities based on new technology that helps us to leapfrog the competition. In this vein, we adopted an Agile development methodology, and more specifically Scrum/XP practices as the key vehicles to achieve this goal

Our development teams transitioned to Agile in 2005. Engaging many of the most well-known experts and coaches in the community, we undertook an accelerated approach to absorbing and incorporating new practices. We saw significant improvement over our previous waterfall methods almost immediately and our enthusiasm for Agile continued to grow. By September 2011 we had a mature Agile development program, having adopted most Scrum and XP practices. Our Scrum teams included all roles (product owners, Scrum masters, business analysts, developers and testers). We had a mature product backlog and ran 30-day sprints with formal sprint planning, reviews, and retrospectives. We were releasing large batches of new features and enhancements once a year (mostly because that is the frequency at which we've always released). Practices such as CI, TDD, story-driven development, continuous customer interaction, pair programming, planning poker, and relative point-based estimation were for the most part well integrated into our teams and process. Our experience showed that Scrum and Agile practices vastly improved collaboration across roles, improved customer functionality, improved code quality and speed.

Our Scrum process includes all analysis, development and testing of features. A feature is declared "done" only once it has passed validation testing in a fully integrated environment performed by a Test Engineer within each Scrum Team. Once all release features are complete, Siemens performs another round of regression testing, followed by customer beta testing before declaring general availability and shipping to all our customers.

Despite many improvements and real benefits realized by our Agile adoption, our overall success was limited. We were continually challenged to estimate and deliver on committed release dates. Meeting regulatory requirements and customer expectations requires a high degree of certainty and predictability. Our internal decision checkpoints and quality gates required firm commitments. Our commitment to customers, internal stakeholder expectations and revenue forecasts required accurate release scope and delivery forecasts that carry a very high premium for delay.

At the program and team levels, sprint and release deadlines were characterized by schedule pressure often requiring overtime and the metrics we collected were not providing the transparency needed to clearly gauge completion dates or provide actionable insight into the state of our teams.

In the trenches, our teams were also challenged to plan and complete stories in time-boxed sprint increments. The last week of each sprint was always a mad rush by teams to claim as many points as possible, resulting in hasty and over-burdened story testing. While velocity rates at sprint reviews often seemed good, reality pointed to a large number of stories blocked or incomplete and multiple features in progress with few, if any, features completing until end of the release. This incongruity between velocity (number of points completed in a sprint) and reality was primarily caused by teams starting too many features and/or stories. It had been common practice to start multiple features at one time to mitigate possible risks. In addition, whenever a story or feature was blocked (for a variety of reasons such as waiting for a dependency from another team, waiting for customer validation, inability to test because of environmental or build break issues, etc.), teams would simply start the next story or feature so that we could claim the points which we had committed to achieve. So, while velocity burn-ups could look in line with expectations, multiple features were not being completed on any regular cadence, leading to bottlenecks especially at the end of the release as the teams strove to complete and test features. During this period we operated under the assumption that if we mastered Agile practices, planned better, and worked harder we would be successful. Heroic efforts were expected.

In November of 2011 executive management chartered a small team of director level managers to coordinate and drive process improvement across the PLM organization, with the key goal of finally realizing the predictability, operational efficiency, and quality gains originally promised by our Agile approach. After some research, the team concluded that any changes had to be systemic. Other previous process improvements had focused on specific functional areas such as coding or testing, and had not led to real improvements across the whole system or value stream. By value stream in this context we mean all development activities performed within the Scrum Teams from "specifying to done". By reviewing the value stream with a "Lean" perspective we realized that our problems were indeed systemic, caused by our predilection for large batch sizes such as large feature releases. Reading Goldratt (Goldratt, 2004), and Reinertsen (Reinertsen, 2009) we also came to understand the impacts of large, systemic queues. Coming to the understanding that the overtime, for which programmers were sacrificing their weekends, may actually have been elongating the release completion date was an epiphany.

This path inevitably led us to learn about Kanban. We saw in Kanban a means of enforcing Lean and continuous improvement across the system while still maintaining our core Agile development practices. Kanban would manage Work In Progress, Cycle Time, and Throughput by providing a pull system and thus reduce the negative impacts of large batches and high capacity utilization. Furthermore, we saw in Kanban the potential for metrics that were both tangible (and could be well understood by all corporate stake-holders) and provide individual teams and program management with data that is highly transparent and actionable.

We chose our revenue-cycle application as our pilot, consisting of 15 Scrum teams located in Malvern, PA., Brooklyn, N.Y., and Kolkata, India. Although each Scrum team focuses on specific business domains, the application itself requires integrating all these domains into a single unitary customer solution. At this scale of systemic complexity, dependency management, and continuous integration, a very high degree of consistency and cohesion across the whole program is required.

With this in mind, we designed a "big-bang" approach with a high degree of policy, work-unit, workflow, doneness, and metric standardization across all teams. We also concluded that we needed electronic boards: large monitors displayed in each team room that would be accessible in real time to all our local and offshore developers. An electronic board would also provide an enterprise management view across the program and a mechanism for real-time metrics collection. Our initial product release using Kanban began in April 2012 and was completed that December. Results from our first experience using Kanban were far better than any of our previous releases. Our Cycle Time looked predictable and defects were down significantly.

Our second release began in March 2013 and finished in September of that same year. We continue to use Kanban for our product development today. As we had hoped, learnings and experience from the first release led to even better results in the releases that followed.

Actionable Metrics

Now that we had decided to do Kanban at Siemens HS, we had to change the metrics we used so that we could more readily align with our newfound emphasis on flow. The metrics of flow are very different than traditional Scrum-style metrics. As mentioned earlier, instead of focusing on things like story points and velocity, our teams now paid attention to Work In Progress (WIP), Cycle Time, and Throughput. The reason these flow metrics are preferable to traditional Agile metrics is because they are much more actionable and transparent. By transparent we mean that the metrics provide a high degree of visibility into the teams' (and programs') progress. By actionable, we mean that the metrics themselves will suggest the specific team interventions needed to improve the overall performance of the process.

To understand how flow metrics might suggest improvement interventions we must first explore some definitions. For Siemens HS, we defined WIP to be any work item (e.g., user story, defect, etc.) that was between the "Specifying Active" step and the "Done" step in our workflow (Figure 17.1).

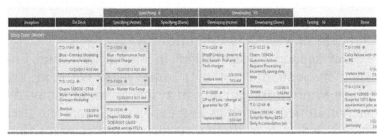

Figure 17.1: Example Kanban Board

Cycle Time was defined to be the amount of total elapsed time needed for a work item to get from "Specifying Active" to "Done". Throughput was defined as the number of work items that entered the "Done" step per unit of time (e.g., user stories per week).

We have stressed throughout this paper that predictability is of paramount importance to Siemens HS. So how was the organization doing before Kanban?

Figure 17.2 is a Scatterplot of Cycle Times for finished stories in the Financials organization for the whole release before Kanban was introduced.

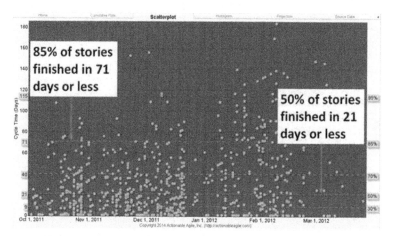

Figure 17.2: Cycle Times in the Release before Kanban

What this Scatterplot tells us is that in this release, 50% of all stories finished in 21 days or less. But remember we told you earlier that Siemens HS was running 30 day sprints? That means that any story that started at the beginning of a sprint had little better than 50% chance of finishing within the sprint. Furthermore, 85% of stories were finishing in 71 days or less—that is 2.5 sprints! What's worse is that Figure 17.3 shows us that over the course of the release the general trend of story Cycle Times was getting longer and longer and longer.

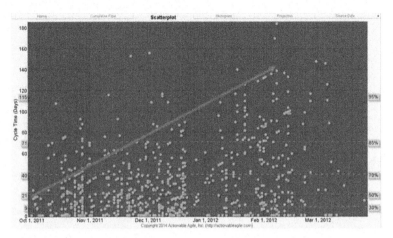

Figure 17.3: General Upward Trend of Cycle Times before the Introduction of Kanban

Figure 17.3 is not a picture of a very predictable process.

So what was going on here? A simplified interpretation of Little's Law tells us that if Cycle Times are too long, then we essentially have two options: decrease WIP or increase Throughput. Most managers inexplicably usually opt for the latter. They make teams work longer hours (stay late) each day. They make teams work mandatory weekends. They try and steal resources from other projects. Some companies may even go so far as to hire temporary or permanent staff. The problem with trying to impact Throughput in these ways is that most organizations actually end up increasing WIP faster than they increase Throughput. If we refer back to Little's Law, we know that if WIP increases faster than Throughput, then Cycle Times will only increase. Increasing WIP faster than increasing Throughput only exacerbates the problem of long Cycle Times.

Our choice (eventually) was the much more sensible and economical one: reduce Cycle Times by limiting WIP through the use of Kanban. What most people fail to realize is that limiting WIP can be as simple as making sure that work is not started at a faster rate than work is completed (please see Figure 5.5 as an example of how mismatched arrival and departure rates increases WIP in the process). Matching arrival rates to departure rates is the necessary first step to stabilizing a system. Only by operating a stable system could we hope to achieve our goal of predictability.

Unfortunately for us, however, the first release that we implemented Kanban, we chose not to limit WIP right away (the argument could be made that we were not actually doing "Kanban" at that point). Why? Because early on in our Kanban adoption the teams and management resisted the imposition of WIP limits. This was not unexpected, as mandating limits on work went against the grain of the then current beliefs. We therefore decided to delay until the third month of the release. This allowed the teams and management to gain a better familiarity of the method and become more amenable.

The delay in implementing WIP limits cost us and in retrospect we should have pushed harder to impose WIP limits from the outset. As you might expect, because of the lack of WIP limits, the very same problems that we saw in the previous release (pre-Kanban) started to appear: Cycle Times were too long and the general trend was that they were getting longer.

Taking a look at the CFD (Figure 17.4) in the first release with Kanban clearly shows how our teams were starting to work on items at a faster rate than we were finishing them:

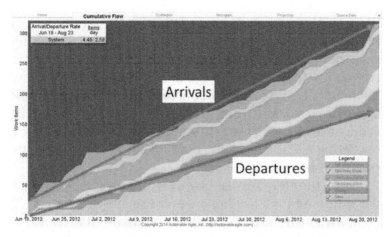

Figure 17.4: CFD Early on in the first release with Kanban

This disregard for when new work should be started resulted in an inevitable increase in WIP which, in turn, manifested itself in longer Cycle Times (as shown in Figure 17.5).

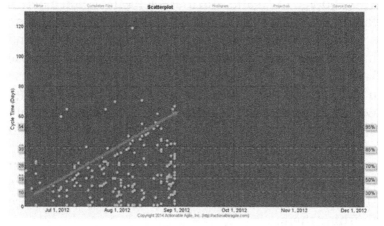

Figure 17.5: Scatterplot early on in the first release with Kanban

Upon seeing these patterns emerge, we instituted a policy of limiting WIP across all teams. Limiting WIP had the almost immediate effect of stabilizing the system such that Cycle Times no longer continued to grow (as shown in Figure 17.6).

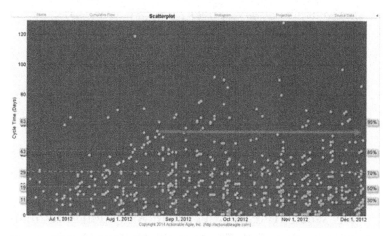

Figure 17.6: Stabilized Cycle Times after introducing WIP Limits

Over the course of our first release with Kanban, the 85th percentile of story Cycle Time had dropped from 71 days to 43 days. And, as you can see from comparing Figure 17.4 to Figure 17.7 (the release before Kanban, and the first release using Kanban, respectively) the teams were suffering from much less variability. Less variability resulted in more predictability. In other words, once we limited WIP in early September 2012 the process Cycle Times did not increase indefinitely as they did the release before. They reached a stable state at about 41 days almost immediately, and stayed at that stable state for the rest of the release.

This stabilization effect of limiting WIP is also powerfully demonstrated in the CFD (Figure 17.7):

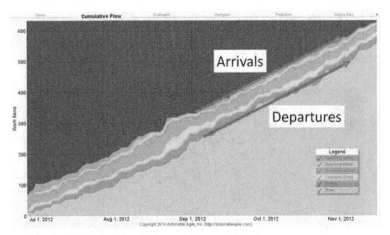

Figure 17.7: CFD in the First Release with Kanban after WIP limits were introduced

The second release after the introduction of Kanban saw much the same result (with regard to predictability). 85 percent of stories were finishing within 41 days and variability was still better controlled. Looking at the two Scatterplots side by side bears this out (Figure 17.8):

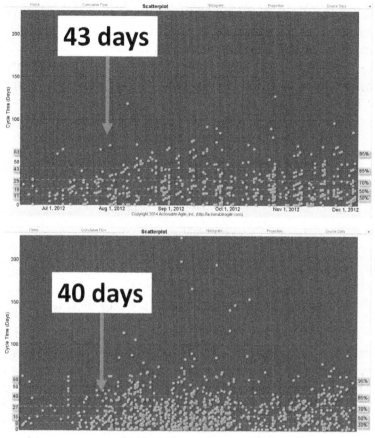

Figure 17.8: Scatterplots of the First Release using Kanban (above) and the Second Release of Kanban (below)

Hopefully it is obvious to the reader that by taking action on the metrics that had been provided, we had achieved our goal of predictability. As shown in Figure 17.8, our first release using Kanban yielded Cycle Times of 43 days or less, and our second release using Kanban yielded Cycle Times of 40 days or less. This result is the very definition of predictability.

By attaining predictable and stable Cycle Times we

would now be able to use these metrics as input to future projections. How we did projections will be discussed in more detail in the next section of this chapter.

These shorter Cycle Times and decreased variability also led to a tremendous increase in quality (Figure 17.9):

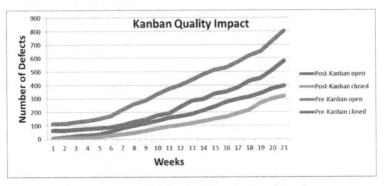

Figure 17.9: Quality Compared between Releases

Figure 17.9 shows how Kanban both reduced the number of defects created during release development well as minimizing the gap between defects created and defects resolved during the release. By managing queues, limiting work-in progress and batch sizes and building a cadence through a pull system (limited WIP) versus push system (non-limited WIP) we were able to expose more defects and execute more timely resolutions. On the other hand "pushing" a large batch of requirements and/or starting too many requirements will delay discovery of defects and other issues; as defects are hidden in incomplete requirements and code.

By understanding Little's Law, and by looking at how the flow appears in charts like CFDs and Scatterplots, Siemens HS could see what interventions were necessary to get control of their system. Namely, the organization was suffering from too much WIP which was, in turn, affecting Cycle Time and quality. In taking the action to limit WIP, Siemens saw an immediate decrease in Cycle Time and an immediate increase in quality.

These metrics also highlighted problems within the Siemens HS product development process, and the following section of this chapter will discuss what next steps the organization is going to implement in order to continue to improve its system.

How Metrics Changed Everything

Apart from the improvements in predictability and quality, we also saw significant improvements in operational efficiency. We had "real-time" insight into systemic blocks, variability and bottlenecks and could take appropriate actions quickly. In one case by analyzing Throughput (story run rate) and Cycle Time for each column (specifying, testing and developing), we were able to clearly see where we were experiencing capacity problems. We were also able to gauge our "flow efficiency" by calculating the percentage of time stories were being worked on or "touched" versus "waiting" or "blocked". Wait time is the time a story sits in an inactive or done queue because moving to the next active state is prevented by WIP limits. Blocked time is the time work on a story is impeded, including impediments such as build-breaks, defects, waiting for customer validation etc. The calculation is made by capturing time spent in the "specifying done and developing done" column plus any additional blocked time which we call "wait time". (Blocked or impediment data is provided directly by the tool we are using). Subtracting "wait time" from total Cycle Time gives us "touched time". Calculating flow efficiency is simply calculating the percentage of total touch time over total Cycle Time. Flow efficiency percentage can act as a powerful Key Performance Indicator (KPI) or benchmark in terms of measuring overall system efficiency.

This level of transparency, broadly across the program and more deeply within each team enabled us to make very timely adjustments. Cumulative flow diagrams provided a full picture at the individual team and program levels where our capacity weaknesses lay and revealed where we needed to make adjustments to improve Throughput and efficiency. For example, at the enterprise level using the Cumulative Flow Diagram the management team was able to see higher Throughput in *"developing"* versus *"testing"* across all teams and thus make a decision to invest in increasing test automation exponentially to re-balance capacity. This was actually easy to spot as the *"developing done"* state on the CFD consistently had stories queued up waiting for the "testing" column WIP limits to allow them to move into *"testing"*. At the team level the metrics would be used to manage WIP by adjusting WIP limits when needed to ensure flow and prevent the build-up of bottlenecks and used extensively in retrospectives to look at variability. By using the Scatterplot, teams could clearly see stories whose Cycle Time exceeded normal ranges, perform root cause analysis and take steps and actions to prevent recurrence. The CFD also allowed us to track our average Throughput or departure-rate (the number of stories we were completing per day/week etc.) and calculate an end date based on the number of stories remaining in the backlog – (similar to the way one uses points and velocity, but more tangible). Furthermore by controlling WIP and managing flow we saw continued clean builds in our continuous integration process, leading to stable testing environments, and the clearing of previously persistent testing bottlenecks.

The results from the first release using Kanban were better than expected. The release completed on schedule and below budget by over 10%. The second release was even better: along with sustained improvements in Cycle Time, we also became much faster. By reducing Cycle Time we were increasing Throughput, enabling us to complete 33% more stories than we had in the previous release, with even better quality in terms of number of defects and *first pass yield* – meaning the percentage of formal integration and regression tests passing the first time they are executed. In the release prior to Kanban our first pass yield percentage was at 75%, whereas in the first Kanban release the pass percentage rose to 86% and reached 95% in our second release using Kanban.

The metrics also gave us a new direction in terms of release forecasting. By using historical Cycle Times we could perform Monte-Carlo simulation modelling to provide likely completion date forecasts. If these forecasts proved reliable, we would no longer need to estimate. In our second Kanban release we adopted this practice along with our current points and velocity estimation planning methods and compared the results. Apart from the obvious difference in the use of metrics versus estimated points, the simulation provides a distribution of likely completion timeframes instead of an average velocity linear based forecast – such as a burn up chart. Likewise Cycle Time metrics are not based on an average (such as average number of points) but on distributions of actual Cycle Times. The Histogram in Figure 17.10 is an example of actual historical Cycle Time distributions that Siemens uses as input to the modelling tool. In this example 30% of stories accounting for 410 actual stories had Cycle Times of 9 days or less, the next 20% accounting for 225 stories had Cycle Times of 10 to 16 days and so forth.

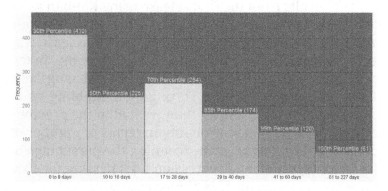

Figure 17.10: Cycle Time Distributions

What we learned was that velocity forecasts attempt to apply a deterministic methodology to an inherently uncertain problem. That type of approach never works. By using the range or distributions of historical Cycle Times from the best to worst cases and simulating the project hundreds of times, the modelling simulation provides a range of probabilistic completion dates at different percentiles. For example see Figure 17.11 below showing likely completion date forecasts used in release planning. Our practice is to commit to the date which is closest to the 85th percent likelihood as is highlighted in the chart. As the chart shows we are also able to use the model to calculate likely costs at each percentile.

Likelihood	Date	Workdays	Cost	Cost of Delay	Days of Delay	L
100.00 %	01-Nov-2013	200	$1,200,000.00	$0.00	0	0
99.20 %	29-Oct-2013	197	$1,182,000.00	$0.00	0	0
95.20 %	25-Oct-2013	193	$1,158,000.00	$0.00	0	0
90.40 %	21-Oct-2013	189	$1,134,000.00	$0.00	0	0
86.80 %	17-Oct-2013	185	$1,110,000.00	$0.00	0	0
79.20 %	13-Oct-2013	181	$1,086,000.00	$0.00	0	0
75.60 %	10-Oct-2013	178	$1,068,000.00	$0.00	0	0
72.00 %	06-Oct-2013	174	$1,044,000.00	$0.00	0	0
69.60 %	02-Oct-2013	170	$1,020,000.00	$0.00	0	0
62.80 %	28-Sep-2013	166	$996,000.00	$0.00	0	0
52.00 %	24-Sep-2013	162	$972,000.00	$0.00	0	0
48.00 %	21-Sep-2013	159	$954,000.00	$0.00	0	0
41.60 %	17-Sep-2013	155	$930,000.00	$0.00	0	0
32.80 %	13-Sep-2013	151	$906,000.00	$0.00	0	0

Figure 17.11: Result of Monte-Carlo simulation showing probability forecast at different percentages

Over the course of the release the model proved extremely predictive; moreover, it also provided to Siemens the ability to perform ongoing risk analysis and "what-if" scenarios with highly instructive and reliable results. For example, in one case, to meet an unexpected large scope increase on one of the teams, the Program Management Team was planning to add two new Programmers. The modelling tool pointed to adding a Tester to the team rather than adding programming. The tool proved very accurate in terms of recommending the right staffing capacity to successfully address this scope increase.

At the end of the day, it was an easy decision to discard story point velocity based estimation and move to release completion date forecasts. The collection of historical Cycle Time metrics that were stable and predictable enabled Siemens to perform Monte-Carlo simulations, which provided far more accurate and realistic release delivery forecasts. This was a huge gap in our Agile adoption closed. In analyzing the metrics, Siemens also discovered that there was no correlation between story point estimates and actual Cycle Time.

Siemens also gained the ability to more accurately track costs; as we discovered that we could in fact correlate Cycle Time to actual budgetary allocations. Siemens could now definitively calculate the unit costs of a story, feature and/or a release. By using the modelling tool we could now forecast likely costs along with dates. Moreover, we could put an accurate dollar value on reductions or increases in Cycle Times.

The metrics also improved communication with key non PLM stake-holders. It had always been difficult translating relative story points to corporate stakeholders who were always looking for time based answers and who found our responses based on relative story points confusing. Metrics such as Cycle Time and Throughput are very tangible and especially familiar in a company such as Siemens with a large manufacturing sector.

Implementing Kanban also had a positive impact on employee morale. Within the first month, Scrummasters reported more meaningful stand-ups. This sentiment was especially expressed and emphasized by our offshore colleagues, who now felt a much higher sense of inclusion during the stand-up. Having the same board and visualization in front of everyone made a huge difference on those long distant conference calls between colleagues in diametrically opposed time zones. While there was some skepticism as expected, overall comments from the teams were positive; people liked it. This was confirmed in an anonymous survey we did four months into the first release that we used Kanban: the results and comments from employees were overwhelmingly positive. Furthermore, as we now understood the impact of WIP and systemic variability, there was less blame on performance and skills of the team. The root of our problem lay not in our people or skills, but in the amount of Work In Progress.

Conclusion

Kanban augmented and strengthened our key Agile practices such as cross-functional Scrum teams, story driven development, continuous integration testing, TDD, and most others. It has also opened the way to even greater agility through our current plan to transition to continuous delivery.

Traditional Agile metrics had failed Siemens HS in that we did not provide the level of transparency required to manage software product development at this scale. Looking at a burn-down chart showing average velocity does not scale to this level of complexity and risk. This had been a huge gap in our Agile adoption which was now solved.

Understanding flow—and more importantly understanding the metrics of flow—allowed Siemens to take specific action in order improve overall predictability and process performance. On this note, the biggest learning was understanding that predictability was a systemic behavior that one has to manage by understanding and acting in accordance with the assumptions of Little's law and the impacts of resource utilization.

Achieving a stable and predictable system can be extremely powerful. Once you reach a highly predictable state by aligning capacity and demand; you are able to see the levers to address systemic bottle-necks and other unintended variability. Continuous improvement in a system that is unstable always runs the risk of improvement initiatives that result in sub-optimizations.

The extent of the improvement we achieved in terms of overall defect rates was better than expected. Along with the gains we achieved through managing WIP; we had placed significant focus on reinforcing and improving our CI and quality management practices. Each column had its own doneness criteria and by incorporating "doneness procedures" into our explicit policies we were able to ensure that all quality steps were followed before moving a story to the next column – for example moving a story from "Specifying" to "Developing". Most of these practices had predated Kanban; however the Kanban method provided more visibility and rigor.

The metrics also magnified the need for further improvement steps: The current Kanban implementation incorporates activities owned within the Scrum Teams; but does not extend to the "backend process" – regression testing, beta testing, hosting, and customer implementation. Like many large companies Siemens continues to maintain a large batch release regression and beta testing process. Thus begging the question; what if we extended Kanban across the whole value stream from inception to implementation at the customer? Through the metrics, visualization, managing WIP and continuous delivery we could deliver value to our customers faster and with high quality. We could take advantage of Kanban to manage flow, drive predictable customer outcomes, identify bottle-necks and drive Lean continuous improvement through the testing, operations and implementation areas as well. In late 2013 we began our current and very ambitious journey to extend the

Kanban method across the whole value stream.

Finally it is important to say that the use of metrics instead of estimation for forecasting has eliminated the emotion and recrimination associated with estimation. Anyone wishing to go back to estimating sprints would be few and far between, including even those who had previously been the most skeptical.

Key Learnings and Takeaways

- Traditional Agile metrics were not working for Siemens HS as those metrics did not provide the transparency and predictability required by Siemens HS' customers and management.
- Siemens HS decided to dump Story Points and Velocity in favor of WIP, Cycle Time, and Throughput.
- After that shift, Siemens HS quickly discovered the root of their problem was not people or skillsets but too much WIP.
- By controlling WIP, Siemens HS was able to reduce Cycle Time from 71 days at the 85th percentile to 43 days at the 85th percentile.
- Controlling WIP also increased the quality of the HS releases dramatically.
- The second release after limiting WIP produced story Cycle Times of 40 days at the 85th percentile.
- Having predictable Cycle Times allowed Siemens to mostly abandon their old estimation practices.
- The use of metrics instead of estimation for forecasting has eliminated the emotion and recrimination associated with estimation.
- Predictable Cycle Times have also allowed Siemens HS to begin to utilize more advanced forecasting techniques like the Monte Carlo Method.

Acknowledgements

As any author will tell you, there may be one name on the front cover, but a book is only possible due to the hard work of numerous people. If I may, I'd like to call your particular attention to the efforts of the few of those listed here.

First, I have to say there is no one in the software industry who understands the principles of flow and how to apply those principles to teams better than **Frank Vega**. If you want to know anything about flow metrics and analytics, Frank is the guy to ask—which I did on way too many occasions, I'm sure. When reviewing this book, his comments were insightful, thought-provoking, and pragmatic. He is one of the few people whose opinion I implicitly trust on this stuff.

I'm not sure there is anyone in the Agile community who asks tougher questions than **Nannette Brown**. She constantly challenged me to come up with better answers and was (is) never satisfied until I did.

To **Mike Longin** and **Prateek Singh** I have to say thanks for your willingness to learn and provide valuable feedback on how to introduce these concepts to teams. We've got much more work to do!

Arin Sime is one of the few truly great minds in in all of Agile. Thanks for giving me the opportunity to share my ideas.

Troy Tuttle has built one of the greatest Lean communities from scratch and, more importantly, has allowed me to contribute when I can. The whole Lean-Agile movement would be a much better place with more people like Troy.

Steve Reid refuses to allow his organization to stagnate. In his mind there is always room for improvement and to his great credit he allows his team members the room to experiment and innovate. Thanks, Steve, for letting me be a part of that ride.

Dennis Kirlin is one of those guys who you can sit down with and solve world hunger over a cup of coffee—or a whisky as the case may be. There is a reason his Agile teams are the envy of his whole city.

For those of you who don't know, **Darren Davis** is the true "Father of Kanban". It was his matter-of-fact approach to solving real-world problems that got the movement off of the ground. I was fortunate enough to learn from him as he guided me through the process of shedding the shackles of sprints. Because of him I've never looked back.

A special thanks to **Troy Magennis** for two reasons. First, for daring the community to get out of its comfort zone and think about the world more probabilistically; and, second, for his gracious permission to let me use his Monte Carlo Simulation tool to run my crazy experiments. I've mentioned this before, but I'll say it again: if you don't know about Troy's work then you need to look him up.

Bennet Vallet is one of those rare individuals who constantly—and I mean constantly—pushes himself to learn and get better. Combine that with his willingness to do whatever is needed to get the correct result and you get a formidable force. He has been and continues to be a great mentor to me. Without his prodding this book may never have seen the light of day. True to form, he is already asking for the next version that covers the more advanced topics.

Vanessa Vacanti is the James Brown of knowledge work. She constantly reminded me to keep this material in the realm of the practical. Thanks for all of your help, LEHjr!

To my twin sister, **Dina Vacanti**. You don't get to choose your siblings, but if I could, I would choose you every time.

Al and **Pat Vacanti** are the whole reason I was able to write this book. How do you ever say thanks enough for that?

As always, **Todd Conley** remains my wizard behind the curtain. Todd never wavered in his belief when I first pitched the idea of a flow analytics tool to him two years ago, and he has been tireless in his pursuit of perfection in developing that product ever since. Todd has a no-nonsense approach to building software and is without a doubt the best developer I have ever known. He is a trusted advisor, invaluable colleague, and great friend.

Last, but absolutely not least, I'd like to thank my wife, **Ann**. For her role in all of this, she deserves top billing and the "and". She deserves the EGOT. For putting up with me, she deserves both the Nobel Prize and sainthood. No matter how preoccupied, absent-minded, or just plain stupid I've been she has always supported me. In the whole time that I've known her, whenever I've wanted to take risks both professionally and personally, she has never said no. I can't imagine a better partner. Nor would I want to.

All of the people listed above have been great collaborators for me. If this book falls short then I can't fault any of them. That blame lies solely with me.

And, lastly, to you, the reader. Thanks for reading!

Daniel S. Vacanti

March 2015

Bibliography

Bertsimas, D., D. Nakazato. *The distributional Little's Law and its applications.* Operations Research. 43(2) 298–310, 1995.

Brumelle, S. *On the relation between customer and time averages in queues.* J. Appl. Probab. 8 508–520, 1971.

Deming, W. Edwards. *The New Economics.* 2nd Ed. The MIT Press, 1994

Deming, W. Edwards. *Out of the Crisis.* The MIT Press, 2000.

Glynn, P. W., W. Whitt. *Extensions of the queueing relations $L = \lambda W$ and $H = \lambda G$.* Operations Research. 37(4) 634–644, 1989.

Goldratt, Eliyahu M., and Jeff Cox. *The Goal.* 2nd Rev. Ed. North River Press, 1992.

Heyman, D. P., S. Stidham Jr. *The relation between customer and time averages in queues.* Oper. Res. 28(4) 983–994, 1980.

Hopp, Wallace J., and Mark L. Spearman. *Factory Physics.* Irwin/McGraw-Hill, 2007.

Hubbard, Douglas W. *How to Measure Anything: Finding the Value of Intangibles In Business.* John Wiley & Sons, Inc., 2009.

Little, J. D. C. *A proof for the queuing formula: $L = \lambda W$.* Operations Research. 9(3) 383–387, 1961.

Little, J. D. C., and S. C. Graves. "Little's Law." D. Chhajed, T. J. Lowe, eds. *Building Intuition: Insights from Basic Operations Management Models and Principles.* Springer Science + Business Media LLC, New York, 2008.

Magennis, Troy. *Forecasting and Simulating Software Development Projects.* Self-published, 2011.

Reinertsen, Donald G. *Managing the Design Factory*. Free Press, 1997.

Reinertsen, Donald G. *The Principles of Product Development Flow*. Celeritas Publishing, 2009.

Ries, Eric. *The Lean Startup*. Crown Business, 2011.

Roubini, Nouriel, and Stephen Mihm. *Crisis Economics*. Penguin Books, 2010.

Savage, Sam L. *The Flaw of Averages*. John Wiley & Sons, Inc., 2009.

Shewhart, W. A. *Economic Control of Quality of Manufactured Product*, 1931.

Shewhart, W. A. *Statistical Method from the Viewpoint of Quality Control*, 1939.

Stidham, S., Jr. *L = λ W: A discounted analogue and a new proof.* Operations Research. 20(6) 1115–1126, 1972.

Stidham, S., Jr. *A last word on L= λ W*. Operations Research. 22(2) 417–421, 1974.

Vacanti, Daniel S. and Bennet Vallet. "Actionable Metrics at Siemens Health Services". *AgileAlliance.com. 1 Aug 2014.*

Vallet, Bennet. "Kanban at Scale: A Siemens Success Story." *Infoq.com.* 28 Feb 2014.

Vega, Frank. "Are You Just an Average CFD User?" *Vissinc.com.* 21 Feb 2014.

Vega, Frank. "The Basics of Reading Cumulative Flow Diagrams". *Vissinc.com.* 29 Sep 2011.

Wheelan, Charles. *Naked Statistics*. W. W. Norton & Company, 2013.

Wheeler, Donald J., and David S. Chambers. *Understanding Statistical Process Control*. 2nd Ed. SPC Press, 1992.

Wikipedia "Monte Carlo method." *Wikipedia.com* 01 Aug 2014.

Wikipedia "Uniform Distribution." *Wikipedia.com* 01 Aug 2014.

305

Wikipedia "Uniform Distribution (discrete)." *Wikipedia.com* 01 Aug 2014.

About the Author

Daniel Vacanti is a 20-year software industry veteran who got his start as a Java Developer/Architect and who has spent most of the last 15 years focusing on Lean and Agile practices. In 2007, he helped to develop the Kanban Method for knowledge work. He managed the world's first project implementation of Kanban that year, and has been conducting Kanban training, coaching, and consulting ever since. In 2011 he founded Corporate Kanban, Inc., which provides world-class Lean training and consulting to clients all over the globe–including several Fortune 100 companies. In 2013 he co-founded ActionableAgile™ which provides industry leading predictive analytics tools and services to any Lean-Agile process. Daniel holds a Masters in Business Administration and regularly teaches a class on lean principles for software management at the University of California Berkeley.

Made in the USA
Monee, IL
11 February 2020

21637485R00174